THE COMPACT HISTORY OF MANKIND

BY

JAMES GAULT

Cover by "GermanCreative", Austria

CONTENTS

INTRODUCTION

Being educated by wiser persons, we know that the Latin term "homo sapiens" literally means "wise man". I sometimes have my doubts about the wisdom of modern man and in my lifetime even the word "man" is oft challenged as sexist. "Personkind" or similar such synonyms sound tortured and universally awful, so until some Wiser Person come up with a readily usable term, "man" and "mankind" are with us yet. What is not yet with us is a capacity to know the future. For those not fixated on the present, there is thus only the past to contemplate, perhaps learn from. Some partly-wise persons believe that by studying that past we can forecast the future. Well, no, we cannot! We can perhaps learn a little about ourselves and our erratic human behaviour, but seeing the future is a role for the mystics.

There is an indefinable yearning in many humans to know where we have come from. In some that is strong – a yearning maybe to belong to a particular tribe. Indeed, we are all to some extent tribal, whether that be a particular sporting team, a family hierarchy or a genetic origin. 'Birds of a feather stick together' as one old saying has it. The discovery of genes and its consequent science of genetics has only arisen in my own limited life span. One day it may be more revealing but until we really understand which came first, the egg or the chicken, we will need to rely on what other partly-wise persons have recorded. What they have already recorded is sometimes disconcerting: our fellow beings have been invading, slaughtering and generally been nasty to each other for millennia. That's not to mention what our forebears did to other species. But, as I have heard modern youth proclaim, it is what it is.

What follows is a journey into the past which continues to the present.

COMMON HISTORICAL TERMS
[to be taken with a grain of salt]

The terms used for various 'ages' of mankind (us partly-wise persons) are largely based upon either the type of artefacts discovered by archaeologists or sociological assessments (how we partly-wise persons behave and interact with each other). They cover an enormous range of differing dates depending upon who is using them and where (geographically) the term is being applied. The following rough guide is just that – rough – but it may help some readers fit events into a reasonable chronology. The dates given are arbitrarily rounded and are given titles in this journey (see chapter headings) that don't always match convention.

ICE AGE   - 26millionBC to present (technically an ice age is a long-term reduction in global temperature with extensive ice sheets – which still exists at present – but some count the age ending at the same time as the last intense cold [or 'glaciation'] period around 7,500BC). Earth is presently in an inter-glacial period although average temperatures have been increasing unusually quickly since 1980.

STONE AGE - 1,000,000BC to 2,000BC – subdivided into:

PALEOLITHIC - 1,000,000BC to 9,000BC

MESOLITHIC - 9,000BC to 5,000BC

NEOLITHIC - 5,000BC to 2,000BC

BRONZE AGE - 2,000BC to 1,000BC

IRON AGE - 1,000BC to 1BC [to much later in some regions]

MIGRATION AGE - 1-500AD [title not conventionally used]

DARK AGE - 500-1000AD [Sometimes aligned with Early Middle Ages]

MIDDLE AGES (MEDIEVAL PERIOD)

EARLY - 400 – 800

MID - 800 – 1500

POST - 1500 – 1800

RENNAISSANCE - 1400 - 1600

AGE OF ENLIGHTENMENT - 1600 – 1800

INDUSTRIAL REVOLUTION - 1760 - 1840

<u>**A perspective**</u>: if the dots on these pages are taken as representing the age of the Earth, then sapient mankind (us) has existed for less than a quarter of the final dot.

....
....
....
....
....
....
....
....
....
....
....
....
....
....
....
....
....
....
....
....
....
....
....

....
....
....
....
....
....
....
....
....
....
....
....
....
....
....
....
....

EACH DOT REPRESENTS SOME ONE MILLION YEARS

SOME BACKGROUND TRIVIA

There are some bits of information that may be considered important to understanding the variety of dates different wiser-persons give to any particular event. Others might consider it trivia, but if I leave it out I risk being hounded by wiser persons than me. So, let's talk about dates – neither the romantic kind nor the fruit but the sort that give us a sort of understandable time-line of events. The predominant calendar in modern use is the solar-based Gregorian calendar of Pope Gregory XIII in 1582. That is itself based upon the Julian calendar [ie of Julius Caesar] introduced in 46BC. That's our starting point for dates – an arbitrary reference point on which to base the rest.

References to BC and AD (respectively before and after the birth of Jesus Christ) are not popular in some circles due to their religious basis. The terms BCE/CE (Common Era) are often substituted. BC & AD have worked well for a couple of thousand years, though, so I am sticking with them. AD (Latin "Anno Domini", year of our Lord) can get a bit tiresome on constant repetition, so I will spare you that: AD is omitted.

There have been many other calendars in use over time and some others are still used, notably the Islamic, Hebrew, Zoroastrian and Hindu calendars. The Islamic (or Hijri) calendar can cause especial confusion as it is lunar based and whilst AH1 equates to Gregorian 622, the years are of different duration and before AH1 years were not numbered at all but named after significant events. The Chinese calendar is different again, operating on a sixty-year cycle. Further, widespread use of the Gregorian calendar is relatively recent: it was adopted by Britain in 1752 but by Turkey and Russia not until 1917 and 1918 respectively. Despite all that, we will stick with it for our purposes.

There is also some risk in attributing ANY precise dates to past events. As one goes back further in time the broader the scope for error. Archaeology is as much art as it is science with much estimation, interpolation, deduction and sheer speculation often involved. Radiometric dating and thermoluminescence add a degree of modern scientific accuracy to some occurrences but not all and with varying degrees of precision. Any dates provided are thus the most accurate identified by this not-so-wise person and there are no guarantees.

On Places.

Your local travel agent would probably look at you rather oddly were you to seek a trip to Mesopotamia or Outremer. These are place-names which, like many others, have no contemporary relevance and are often difficult to place on current maps. Equally modern cities such as London and Tokyo have incurred multiple name changes over the years whilst some ancient towns simply no longer exist. As far as is practical modern place names are used throughout this story whilst historical names, where their use is essential, are supported by a contemporary geographical reference in brackets.

HOME BASE

Mankind's only known habitation has been planet Earth which formed some 4,500 million years ago as a decidedly inhospitable spot. Violently mobile hot molten rock surrounded by an equally violent storm-ridden atmosphere of toxic and sulphurous gases was the likely scenario. It was then closer to our sun and spinning faster than at present. After about 1500 million years 'cyanobacteria' evolved, the significance of which is that these used a form of water-based photosynthesis with oxygen as a by-product. These processes were enormously slow – yet another 1500 million years would pass before fungi formed with any prospect of survival on land and another 700 million years for multi-cellular organisms to appear. At about this stage, some 800 million years ago, Earth was still experiencing land shifts, massive tides and hurricane force winds with the added factor of a 200-million-year global ice age.

It should not be thought, though, that Earth proceeded through some neat linear progression toward its current relatively benign home for mankind. A few key factors were helpful. A surface crust, albeit wrinkled and volcanic, was forming; gaseous condensation produced water; and oxygen levels were slowly rising. Separate land and sea existed. Stability was not, however, the order of the day. Large movements of the tectonic plates, volcanic action and varying CO2 levels together with variations in orbit and tilting of the Earth's axis caused substantial variations in received solar radiation on top of variations in the sun's own solar output. The outcome was enormous and long-lasting variations in climate of orders of magnitude that make contemporary concerns over man-made warming pale into insignificance.

There were five major ice ages, the most significant peaking around 650,000BC and lasting 50,000 years. These periods themselves had variations involving colder (glacial) periods and warmer (interglacial) periods. The glacial periods were not simply "cold weather" – ice would have been nearly 4,000 metres thick in places and sea levels would drop more than 100 metres. The Mediterranean, for example, would once have been a desert. The most recent ice age began some 2.6 million years ago and, as polar ice sheets prevail, technically persists today. Fortuitously for the comfort of contemporary mankind, though, Earth has been experiencing an interglacial period of warmer climate since about 9,700BC.

When global glaciation receded some 600 million years ago, evolution seems to have picked up its pace. Indications of animal life (fossilised footprints) exist from 500 million BC and of seed-bearing plants from 350 million BC. Dinosaurs roamed Earth between around 230 million BC and 66 million BC. Evolutionary processes were severely disrupted at that latter date when a mass extinction of plants and animals occurred, almost certainly caused by a massive (10-15km) asteroid impacting Earth. Life changed dramatically. Perhaps coincidentally, primates (and man is a primate) started to appear. Fossils of early primates in the form of small squirrel-like quadrupeds have been discovered in North America and western Europe dating from around 65 million BC. Grasses (and thus grazing) appeared around 35 million BC. Sapient mankind (us partly-wise persons) remained a somewhat distant prospect but the basis was certainly being laid. Building on that rudimentary basis would take well over another 60 million years before Earth would play host to such creatures. Earth itself would continue to change shape, with North America physically separating from Europe and joining South America whilst the Indian sub-continent was slowly merging with Asia. Australasia drifted slowly away from Antarctica. These tectonic plate movements continue today: not quickly – less than ten centimetres per year – but sufficient to require modern GPS mapping systems to be re-calibrated every few years.

STONE AGE 1 - THE EARLY WALKERS: 70,000-10,000BC

Recent history is littered with discoveries of skeletons and fossils of what may have been our ancestors – or may not. What triggered the development of modern man, by which is meant *"homo sapiens"* (us partly-wise persons or for the purist *'homo sapiens sapiens'*), and when that occurred, evolutionary or otherwise, is simply not known. What is as certain as can reasonably be, though, is that modern mankind did NOT descend from monkeys, apes or even *Neanderthals*. Modern man is distinct, although we do share a small percentage of DNA with *Neanderthals* indicating that some 'cross pollination' occurred early-on, or perhaps also that we share a common ancestor such as *homo heidelbergensis (600,000BC – 200,000BC)*. The same applies to Melanesians and Australian aboriginals who share a small percentage of DNA with *"Denisova Man"* – a different early hominid found in Siberia of all unlikely places. We share much more DNA with chimpanzees (some 98%) but evolutionary divergence would have occurred from a common ancestor some 6 million years ago.

Walking, or bipedalism, is a characteristic feature of humans and is a point of differentiation from apes, whose feet are quite different. It is entirely plausible that members of the hominid family (eg *"australopithecines"*) walked on Earth prior to the emergence of Man – ie hominids of the *"homo"* genus, and specifically *homo sapiens* with whom we are concerned. This would certainly be true of modern man's early human relatives – of which there are at least six species and probably many more. These include *homo erectus* living from before 1million BC to around 70,000BC and *homo neanderthalensis* (Neanderthals) living from 350,000BC to as recently as 30,000BC. There is evidence that a number of different 'homo' species coexisted. All of these species were bipedal, controlled fire, used tools and, progressively, made shelters. Then, about 200,000BC an anatomically different species started to appear – us self-indulgently termed "Wise Man" or *homo sapiens* – initially, probably, in Africa. We do, of course, here continue use of the term "man" apologetically in its gender-neutral sense.

Early *homo sapiens* began to appear in various parts of the world over the next 130,000 years, to varying degrees co-existing, and to a limited extent interbreeding, with other homo species. Then, about 70,000BC things changed dramatically with *homo sapiens* exhibiting significant improvement in communications and mental ability. This is sometimes referred to as the 'cognitive revolution' and triggered the development of needles, bows and arrows, boats, oil lamps and warm clothing together with signs of art, religion and commerce. Within the relatively short space of 40,000 years all other homo species seem to have been replaced, absorbed or hunted out of existence. It was a little like a horse race where one emerges from the field to take a commanding and unassailable lead: he or she seemed to come from nowhere.

Initially, significant expansion of *homo sapiens* (around 70,000BC) seems to have been constrained, possibly by *the Neanderthals*, although genetic studies indicate a total population then of only around 10,000 or less. By 40,000BC a more numerous populace, albeit still 'hunter-gatherers', managed to expand over vast distances and the occupation of Earth by modern partly-wise persons had truly begun.

Survival and expansion were inter-dependent for our foraging forebears of this era. Reliant as they were upon wild plants and even wilder animals, they would have been forced to move further afield whenever local resources became depleted. Shelter would have been opportunistic, or at best temporary, and there was no scope for accumulation of property. Where they went, they walked: what goods they kept, they carried. Patently, though, they did survive – by 10,000BC the population had increased to some 5-8 million – and they certainly expanded – within the same period they were present on every continent on Earth, although Antarctica may be a dubious inclusion.

Rudimentary though their living arrangements were, it would be a mistake to think our predecessors unintelligent. They had to be smart: it is simply that their skills and knowledge were focussed on a rather fundamental issue: survival. To succeed their levels of physical fitness and mental acuity needed to be of the highest order; the knowledge of local fauna and flora comprehensive; and communications ability well practised. We know virtually nothing of their artistic or spiritual aspirations, nor indeed of matters relating to hierarchy or family life which rest largely in the realm of speculation. What we do know from archaeological evidence is that they respected their dead with elaborate burials as early as

28,000BC and were imaginative, as evidenced by a carved half human, half lion ivory figurine discovered in Germany and dated around 35,000BC. The labour involved in carving that work from a Woolly Mammoth tusk with only a flint knife demonstrates remarkable skill, perseverance and artistic capacity. Caves around the world are similarly endowed with artistic endeavours – mainly human hands or animals – some of a similar age – 33-38,000BC.

History has always had its hermits, but by and large humans have always prospered better in shared company, whether that be for security, shared burden, learning or simply procreation. It was thus inevitable that groups would form, varying in size from a family of a score or more to some hundreds. That in turn placed a greater demand upon resources. A further inevitability was that such groups would prefer and succeed better in locations where resources were plentiful, climate equable and geography comfortable. That did present difficulties as the middle of this period, peaking around 18,000BC, was characterised by an ice age with temperatures some 10^0C lower and sea levels around 90 metres lower than at present.

When things began to warm up, albeit very erratically, ice sheets melted and sea levels rose. Toward the end of this period, around 10,000BC, waterside land was disappearing by a little over 20 metres each year. Waterside land retained its attraction, though, as fish were a relatively unthreatening and plentiful food source. The first villages thus included those of fisher-folk but more populous settlements arose in the benign geography of the Tigris/Euphrates/Jordan valleys; Egypt; Turkey; and with settlements built with stone around 12,000BC (Palestine/Israel). Concentrations of humans – of whom there were increasing numbers (some 6 million by 10,000BC) – had both benefits and disadvantages. The former included security and mutual support, including shared labour, whilst the latter encompassed rubbish, vermin and greater demand upon local food resources. Regardless, by 10,000BC human settlements (by way of villages as opposed to caves) were becoming the norm, as was agriculture.

STONE AGE 1 – MILESTONES 70,000 – 10,000BC

70,000BC "Cognitive revolution" occurs: *Homo Sapiens* ("Wise Man") develops new ways of thinking and communicating.

66,000BC Massive Meteor impact on Mexico's Yucatan Peninsula wipes out up to 80% of life on Earth.

40,000BC Neanderthals begin to disappear. Burned remains in S. Australia ("Mungo Man") indicative of cremation.

37,000BC Volcanic "super-eruption" occurs in Italy (Campi Flagres) spewing ash into the stratosphere, cooling European temperature by around 2^0C for 2-3 years and hastening the demise of the European *Neanderthals.*

25,000BC Homo Sapiens has spread through Europe, N Africa, Syria, Siberia, Asia, Australia.

20,000BC Cave paintings in France (Cro-Magnon Man).

Homo sapiens evident in Mexico.

Increase of 11 Deg C in global temperature over next 8-10,000 years.

18,000BC Oceans reach their lowest levels some 130 metres below present.

15,000BC Improved stone tools (polished v chipped) begin to appear.

13,000BC Earliest known human battle (Egypt; site known as "Cemetery 117").

12,000BC Dogs first domesticated about this time. Northern Europe suffers increased glaciation and sudden intense cold for 200 years ("Older Dryas") First human presence evident in N America (Triquet Island, Canada).

10,900BC Another abrupt glaciation and intense cold for 1,200 years over northern hemisphere ("Younger Dryas").

10,500BC Evidence of human settlement in South America.

10,000BC Homo sapiens the sole surviving 'homo' species.

STONE AGE 2 – SETTLEMENT AND AGRICULTURE: 10,000-2,000BC

No startling transformation event occurred in 10,000BC that marked that year as a turning point. Nonetheless, that year serves well as a notable point in history when modern man became more the settler and less the forager. This was a gradual process and varied in pace from region to region but mankind was now embarked on an irreversible process of agricultural settlement. Whether settlement drove agriculture or vice versa is moot, but until mechanisation and mass production eventually intervene, they become inextricably linked. This process of settlement was a footnote to what had been effectively a mass one-way migration: people (we can call them that now as they had no human competitors) spread across the globe in one direction or another and settled: there was little or no 'going back'.

Two factors then became the major 'drivers' of where significant settlements developed: climate and the presence of rivers.

As the intense cold of the "Younger Dryas" ended, Earth began to warm. The progressive effect was a more benign climate for the growth of plants (and thus animals), although benefits were neither universal nor always enduring. Lower-level land became submerged and some areas such as the N. African Sahara progressed from poor grassland in 10,000BC through a period of intense humidity from 8,500BC (which made the Sahara habitable but the

Nile Valley marshy) and then gradual desiccation after about 5,300BC.

The valleys of the Tigris and Euphrates rivers in **Mesopotamia** (Iraq/Syria) plus SE Turkey saw the most significant settlement and early agriculture, although the Levant (eastern Mediterranean) saw the cultivation of cereal crops a little earlier. Cultivation of cereals such as wheat and barley was evident in Mesopotamia from around 9300BC with constructed granaries seen shortly thereafter and by about 7,000BC a fairly wide range of foodstuffs, including onions, garlic, lentils, chickpeas, dates and even lettuce, were being grown. Over the same period native animals such as sheep, goats, donkeys, oxen and pigs were slowly but surely being domesticated. By the end of this period clay was being used for both pottery and figurines, whilst copper was also discovered.

Egypt was largely grassland in 10,000BC. People here were then hunter-gatherers and a pastoral lifestyle (principally cattle-herding) prevailed, intensifying after 8,500BC when monsoonal rains made condition suitable - even in such places as what is today the Libyan Desert. Ironically, those same rains made the Nile Valley virtually uninhabitable until about 5,300BC when the rains dried up and people shifted there from what was rapidly becoming the arid Sahara we know today.

Intensive farming did not begin in **China** until around 7,000BC and was then concentrated around the Yellow River in the north with millet production and, a little later, the Yangtze River in the south where rice was the principal product. Agricultural development here occurred in relative isolation from the rest of the world but still encompassed similar domestication of dogs, pigs and cattle.

The Indus Valley in **India** was slower to see settlement and agriculture, with the latter being evident from about 5,000BC and little in the way of major settlements for another 2,000 years.

Exactly when and where civilization first arose rather depends upon one's definition of that term. By any measure though, Sumer in Mesopotamia (Iraq) must rank as the prime candidate. Blessed with two river systems and an equable climate, the area was populated at a relatively early date (at least by 8,000BC). The area went through the natural progression from hunter-gathering to more sedentary pastoral and agricultural activities until by the middle of the 4th Millennium BC Sumerians had attained a level of sophistication that could only have occurred by means of capable leadership and organisation. Uruk, its first city (although Eridu is a competitor), had all the hallmarks of well-designed mud-brick houses and paved streets with an ordered and seemingly religious populace.

Uruk was not the only population centre in Sumer and indications are of a series of independent city-states, each with a significant population (10,000+) and each separated by marked boundaries and in some cases canals. Temples were evident —and leadership could well have been centred on the priestly class — as was trade and possibly slave labour. These attributes were supported by irrigated agriculture, simple ploughs and wheeled transport together with a written language — a form of cuneiform ("wedge-shaped") script. Similar developments were evident amongst the Akkadians – Sumer's northern neighbours.

Meanwhile in Egypt, as the climate warmed and dried, hunter-gatherers of the grasslands migrated increasingly to the Nile Valley and settled. Communities began to flourish and, whilst herding and farming formed the backbone of these communities, the more settled lifestyle enabled additional skills to develop. By around 3,500BC these people had developed skills of a high order in pottery, metalworking and irrigation with quite sophisticated ornaments being made. Housing was mainly of mud with straw roofing and communities seemed to have operated independently from each other. Toward the end of this period, however, quite rapid development occurred, such that by 3000BC exquisite pottery design together with ivory, silver and copper works and hieroglyphics were in evidence, as was trade with neighbouring regions. Religious practices included formal burial of the dead and society became more cohesive, possibly with a developing hierarchy, albeit separately in each of Upper (southern) and Lower (northern) Egypt.

Independently developing though they were, the geographic proximity to each other of Mesopotamia, the Levant and Egypt would raise the likelihood of some degree of cross-pollination of ideas between them. That would probably also apply to the Indus Valley (India/Pakistan). At that stage no such exchanges were likely with China where societies were developing quite separately, although at an apparently slower pace. By the end of the third millennium BC people in China were cultivating crops (rice in the south, millet to the north); domesticating animals (dogs, pigs, sheep etc); making useful and decorative pottery; and living in large villages with established religious beliefs and practices. As in Mesopotamia and Egypt, a priestly class was forming.

Elsewhere, other than for a few isolated examples, our partly-wise forebears seem to have been content to continue to hunt animals and gather the fruits of the earth. Much depended simply on what their environment provided.

The "Stone Age" encapsulates an enormous timescale and defies a single or simple description of mankind's activities, other than to say that they were scattered and varied in rates of progression toward what we might term "civilization". It would, however, be a rather unwise partly-wise person to consider our Stone Age forebears intellectually deficient. At the beginning they would necessarily have relied solely on instinct and reflex: but they learned. That accumulated knowledge and skill. When passed from one generation to the next, it delivered much progress and formed a basis for our modern societies. Take, for example, "The Hymn to the Nile", a poem written over 4,100 years ago (still technically in the Stone Age) by an informally educated man of reputedly low birth which comprises fourteen intelligent verses of which any modern poet could be proud.

By the end of the Stone Age there were some 27 million of our forebears on the planet.

STONE AGE 2 – MILESTONES 10,000 – 2,000BC

8,000BC - Early settlements in Egypt and Mesopotamia. Jericho (Israel) perhaps first walled town: mudbrick villages become common. Wheat and Barley domesticated in Middle East.

7,500BC - Oceans 30 metres below present levels but rising rapidly as glaciers melt. Village of around 6,000 people living in mud-brick dwellings evident in S. Turkey (Catalhoyuk) located in area favourable for agriculture.

7,000BC - Sheep and dogs had been domesticated in Europe; goat herding & pulse growing spreading. Corn being domesticated in Mexico; copper beating evident in Turkey. Coastal settlements forming in the Levant (Mediterranean coast).

6,500BC - Britain physically separated from mainland Europe; oceans continue to rise. Evidence of large-scale Bison hunting in N. America.

6,000BC - Copper beads in use in Europe. Norse nomads and fishers inhabit Scandinavia (small fishing boats evident). Torres Strait floods/widens separating New Guinea from Australia; pigs domesticated in Iraq.

5,000BC - Farming villages widespread in Europe; formal burials becoming common. Maize and beans being cultivated in the Americas; physical conflicts arise in Mesopotamia; irrigation in use in Mesopotamia and Egypt.

4,000BC - Ocean levels now some 8 metres below present levels, rising slowly. Copper being smelted in Sumer (Mesopotamia/Iraq); meat being cooked and bread baked in Britain.

3,500BC - A developed civilization evident in Mesopotamia: written language, organised streets and wheeled transport, first cities being formed, notably Ur on the Euphrates River.

3,000BC - Earth's population now 10-20 million. A united Egypt enjoys hieroglyphic script, weaving, copper use, reed boats and a developed bureaucracy. Fortified settlements appear in Spain. Phoenicians (from Levant) settle Syria; Crete settled and becomes centre of Aegean (Minoan) civilization.

2,500BC - The Sahara Desert (N Africa) developing due overgrazing. Egypt has a stable society, a calendar of 365 days and had begun building stone pyramids and timber boats. China has a prosperous society with a philosopher Emperor. Conflict arises in Sumer (Mesopotamia/Iraq). India builds cities of brick buildings with sewerage systems.

2,000BC - Maize and sweet potatoes cultivated in the Americas, rice introduced into China from Indus Valley (NW India/Pakistan) to add to domestic sheep, goats, pigs, oxen and grains. Britons build Stonehenge, trade copper and gold with Europe. First library evident in Babylon (Mesopotamia), Phoenicians and Cretans develop multi-masted ships.

THE BRONZE AGE: 2,000-1,000BC

Us partly-wise persons need to remain aware of the arbitrary nature of assigning names to periods of our progress through the ages. One can find a starting point for "the bronze age" as early as 3300BC and an ending around 1200BC. For our own partly-wise purposes it is between 2000BC and 1000BC. In various areas, though, bronze and also iron were already being smelted and both continued to be produced well after this period.

The significance of bronze, an alloy of copper and other metals such as tin, lies in its superior strength and durability: it can more readily be fashioned into hard-wearing goods, including weapons. That required three components: a source of copper, a source of tin, and artisans to produce the end product. Rarely did those three components naturally occur together, and that encouraged the other element of this age: trade. Regrettably, that trade brought two unwanted passengers with it: migration and conflict.

There were four key centres of population and development in this period.

- **<u>Mesopotamia</u>**, based upon the Rivers Tigris and Euphrates. Bronze had been in use in Mesopotamia for many centuries before the nominal start of our Bronze Age which indicates the advanced degree to which this civilisation had developed. The area was earlier divided between Akkadians in the North (capital Akkad) and Sumerians to the South (capital

Uruk) and comprised a series of what were effectively city-states. At the time, Uruk was probably the largest developed urban city anywhere, with a six-mile perimeter wall, internal canals, palaces and designated residential areas. The people relied on both agriculture and trade for their wellbeing and kept records in a written cuneiform (wedge-shaped) language. Both horses and camels had been domesticated. Conflict, though, was incessant throughout Mesopotamia. An Assyrian threat prevailed from the North in the early part of the age and latterly from the Babylonians in the South. The Akkadians were effectively destroyed by a combination of drought and an invasion by Gutians, a nomadic people from the mountains of Zagros (Iran). The greater threat, though, came from Babylon, only established in 1894BC but becoming a powerful empire under its Amorite leader Hammurabi after 1790BC. By 1776BC Babylon was probably the world's largest city. Toward the end of the Bronze Age, even this dynasty had fallen to invasion by an Anatolian people (Asian Turkey) known as the Hittites.

- **China**, based upon the Yellow and Yangtze Rivers. Though isolated from other centres of growth by distance and terrain, China was doing quite well. The Yellow River (named for its abundant suspended silt) proved to be both a blessing and a curse. In benign times agriculture and the nearby tribal groups thrived but, when they occurred, floods would cause widespread devastation.

Accordingly, much of the early Bronze age was taken up with attempts to contain or control that river. Further South the Yangtze area rainfall was more consistent and less problematic. From the Xia Dynasty, which apparently ruled as the Bronze Age began, through the Shang Dynasty that ruled near its end, there was evidently a high degree of stratification in Chinese society, including the use of captive slaves at the bottom of the pile. Cereals, millet and barley were grown and wine and beer also produced. It was a relatively sophisticated society: writing was developed; horses were domesticated and wheeled vehicles used; whilst music and art flourished and highly decorated objects were manufactured. Bronze had been independently developed but was principally used only for ritual vessels and weapons. Buildings, including palaces, remained of wooden construction. Internal conflicts and an oppressive regime ultimately brought the Shang Dynasty undone around 1046BC when the long-lasting Zhou Dynasty began.

- **<u>Indus Valley</u>**, based upon the Indus River. Here the Harappan civilisation flourished over a very wide area encompassing much of modern Afghanistan, Pakistan and North-Western India. Numerous cities were thriving in the early Bronze Age, some of around 50,000 people, and were well planned with effective water and drainage systems. Buildings were largely brick with ordered laneways and walled citadels, whilst wealth was being generated by agricultural surpluses and trade with such places as Mesopotamia. Their metallurgy involved lead, tin, copper and bronze. The area was protected somewhat from hostile inroads by the barrier of the Hindu Kush mountains to the North, although large migrations of Aryan people from Asia (Iran) did occur. Regardless, the civilisation began to crumble in the latter part of the Bronze Age and by its end was virtually extinct, with its population having progressively dispersed to the East and South into India. This was most likely due to a changing climate: the monsoons upon which their agricultural systems relied were progressively moving Southwards with a consequent increase in drought conditions locally.

- **Egypt**, based upon the Nile. Bronze was evident in Egypt at least a millennium before our nominated period which is indicative of the relatively advanced state of their civilisation. With desert to either side, the relatively protected Nile provided a bounty that enabled an agricultural surplus and consequent trade and wealth. Buildings were of stone; paper (papyrus) and written hieroglyphs allowed for a system of records; a calendar of twelve months; polytheistic religion, including the important Osiris and a developing bureaucracy plus varying forms of slave labour all provided a basis for a stable civilisation. That is not to assert that it actually was stable though. Something like eleven separate dynasties ruled Egypt over the course of the Bronze Age and conflict was evident from the beginning with North versus South hostilities continuing until the country was forcibly reunited in 1991BC. Warfare was not confined to its own borders and various Pharaohs sought to dominate both Syria and Canaan (Palestine). The former conflict generated the first recorded formal peace treaty – the Treaty of Kadesh between Ramesses II of Egypt and King Hattasili III of the Hittites, a warlike people from Anatolia (Turkey) who had previously attacked Mesopotamia and Babylon. Another people that Egypt was having difficulties with in this period were the Hyksos, a semitic people of uncertain origin, possibly Western Asia and the Levant (Lebanon/Palestine/Syria). Their arrival in Egypt around 1782BC was progressive and seemingly peaceful, at least initially, but by 1650BC they had accumulated sufficient strength to seize power in Southern Egypt. The Hyksos do not seem to have left any indelible changes to Egyptian culture and were forcibly expelled to the Levant some one hundred years later.

Developments in culture and societal advances were, of course, being made elsewhere than in our partly-wise selection of key centres. The places concerned were natural places of settlement, generated by migration and concentrations of people in areas that could sustain them. During the Bronze Age it is possible to identify some fifty other separate cultures and over 140 kingdoms or city-states. Being only partly-wise we might address just two of those that may be of interest.

- <u>Minoan civilisation</u>. These were a people based largely in coastal Greece and Crete who made great wealth from maritime trade in the Aegean Sea and Mediterranean. Their imports included copper, tin and ivory, whilst exporting timber, wine, olive oil and dyes. They built impressive cities and palaces, used writing and were noted for their artistic frescoes and pottery. The peak of their culture was around 1600BC but around 1500BC a catastrophe, probably the eruption of Thera (Santorini Island) and subsequent tsunami, marked the beginning of its decline such that it could not be regarded as a separate civilisation by 1100BC.

- <u>Judaism</u>. Untangling the origins and development of Judaism and Israel is no simple exercise and quite beyond your mere partly-wise chronicler. One needs to bear in mind that the whole Eastern Mediterranean was at that time a hotbed of warfare, piracy, tribal disputation, minor city-states and unrecorded migrations. A starting point for Judaism is often accepted as being the migration of a man named Abram (later Abraham) from Sumeria to Canaan, probably near Hebron (Palestine), in around 1700BC. One of his offspring was named Jacob and subsequently changed name to Israel: his monotheistic followers thus became Israelites. That name first appears in the records on an Egyptian stele (inscribed pillar) of 1209BC indicating a distinct people. Canaan had previously been dominated by Egypt for some centuries but Egypt had largely withdrawn and many others moved in, including

Hittites and Sea People or Pelesets (Philistines). Canaan was thus a melting pot of cultures with many minor kingdoms. About 1275BC (dates vary widely), as the Hebrew bible would have it, an exodus occurred of captive Israelites from Egypt, numbering many thousands. There is no Egyptian or archaeological record of this occurring but it could explain a significant increase in the Israeli population of Canaan. In any event, the Israelites were sufficiently strong by 1130BC to engage and defeat an alliance of Canaanite kings. The native Canaanites were ultimately supposed (under biblical command) to have been destroyed. DNA has revealed, however, that modern Lebanese are direct descendants of those very Canaanites.

By the end of the Bronze Age our partly-wise forebears numbered some 50 million.

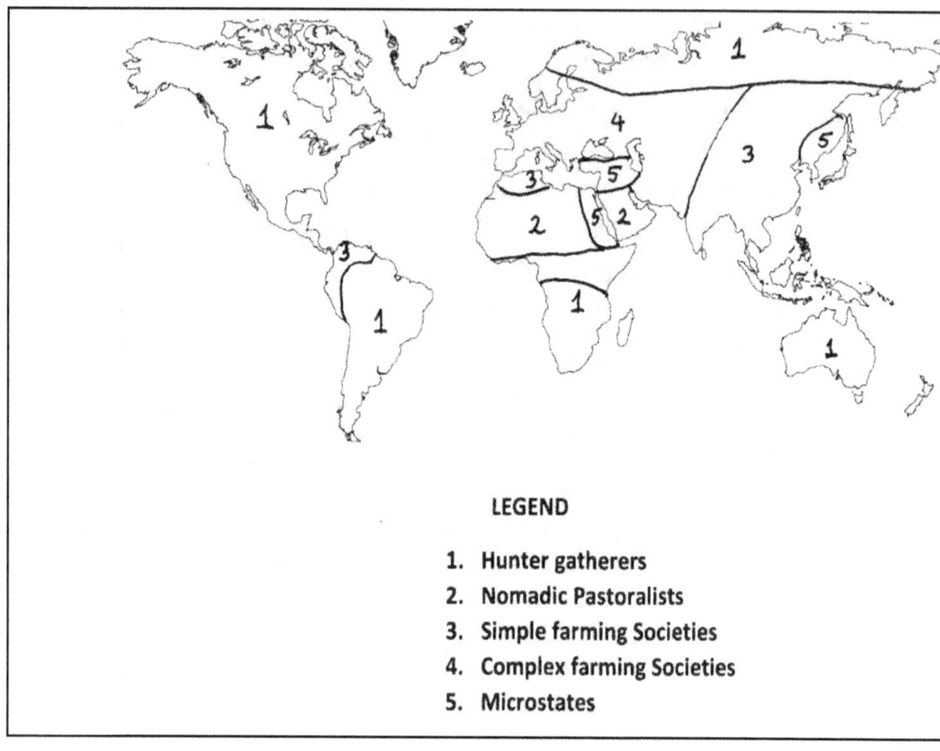

Fig 1: - Indicative state of societal progress by end of the Bronze Age

(Modified from an original work: CC by 2.5)

THE BRONZE AGE – MILESTONES 2000 – 1000BC

2,000BC - Agriculture is developing in central America, the Indus Valley (wheat, barley, apples), India (tea and bananas) and Africa (water melon). Wheat and Barley domesticated in Middle East.

Harappan civilisation in Indus Valley at peak; cities with gridded streets, brick houses and shops, sophisticated sanitation.

1950BC - Amorites, a nomadic Semitic-speaking people spread into Sumeria. Instability evident throughout Mesopotamia.

1894BC - Babylon founded.

1874BC - Pharoah Semansert III constructs canal from River Nile to Red Sea.

1792BC - Hammurabi the Great of Babylon subdues Mesopotamia; introduces Code of Laws.

1782BC - Asiatic Semitic-speaking Hyksos people migrate into Egypt and gain foothold in the North, apparently without bloodshed.

1750BC - Hammurabi the Great dies, Babylonian empire declines.

1700BC - Abram (Abraham) a Sumerian prince, moves to Canaan (Palestine), founds religion which ultimately becomes Judaism.

1630BC - Massive eruption of Mt Thera, Santorini (Greece), widespread tsunami. Minoan (Aegean) civilisation suffers major disruption.

1567BC - Egypt reunited under Pharaoh Ahmose who expels the Hyksos.

1500BC - Norse begin settling on farms, constructing high-stemmed ships. China uses horse-drawn carts; makes silk. Egyptians use geometry.

1300BC - About this time the Hebrew Bible records an exodus of large numbers of captive Israelites from Egypt to Canaan (no archaeological evidence of this).

1258BC - First known (recorded) peace treaty – Egypt and the Hittites at Kadesh (Syria).

1250BC - Battle of Tollense Valley (N Germany), possibly the largest single conflict of the age, involving bronze and wooden weapons and around 4,000 participants.

1200BC - Philistines (probably an Aegean maritime people) settle in Canaan (Palestine/Israel): conflict with Israelites ensues.

1184BC - One of many dates around this time for when legend has it that a Greek army of Agamemnon captures Troy (Trojan war).

1165BC - First recorded workers' strike, apparently over wages, at Thebes (Egypt).

1005BC - King David of Hebron (Palestine) takes Jerusalem, becomes King of Judea.

THE IRON AGE: 1000BC-1BC

Most wise historians would logically assert that the Iron Age began when that metal was first forged in the region being addressed. As that varies immensely across our earth, however, we could (and do) thus have dozens of different periods. In some places such as Australia no Iron Age arose – somewhat ironic as iron ore is that country's principal export in contemporary times. Since we are only partly wise, we will more simply address the Age as comprising the thousand years subsequent to 1000BC.

Bronze can be melted and worked at 1000degC, whereas iron requires 1600degC: the latter thus requires a more advanced furnace. Bronze is denser and stronger than simple iron: easier to cast but harder to forge (beaten into shape). Iron is more brittle and more easily bent but holds its heat longer and is thus more easily worked. A great advance occurred when it was discovered that the addition of a small proportion of carbon to the mix made steel: much stronger and able to hold an edge. The choice of our forebears to shift technology was forced by another element: the disruption of trade. Distant tin supplies from such places as Britain and Afghanistan dried up: iron was the answer.

The availability of iron products enabled more productive agricultural endeavours, thus allowing for less people to be devoted to producing food. Others could then be employed as artisans or soldiers. Those soldiers could then be better armed: steel swords and knives became widely produced – and used. The natural progression of families to form groups and groups to form tribes or ultimately even nations, was evident almost universally. Where the tribe became static, notably in places where agriculture flourished, villages, then towns then cities formed. Many cities became "city-states", protective of their laws, rights and territory. Where that also included expansionist leadership then nation-building began and potentially empires were formed. Conflicts thus became almost inevitable and this was complicated by those tribes that remained pastoralist in nature which required fresh territory whenever over-grazing or inadequate rainfall dictated.

As a broad generalisation our forebears of the Iron Age were superstitious and with few exceptions worshipped a multiplicity of Gods. A priestly class developed, ranging from ascetic Daoshi (Taoists) in China to warlike Celtic Druids and in some cases such as India generated a social order, with priests unsurprisingly at the top. Buddhism also developed in India, Zoroastrianism in Persia. Greece was becoming a font of philosophy, as was China with Confucianism. Knowledge of our Earth was also developing; advanced pottery and ceramics, glassware, astronomy, navigation, medicine all either markedly advanced or originated in this period. There is evidence from Babylonian (Iraqi) tablets, for example, of mathematical calculations of the planet Jupiter's movements made before 50BC.

It would be comforting to think that civilisation was advancing nicely in the Iron Age, but this advance was marred by general behaviours that are a far cry from what we modern partly-wise people could regard as civilised norms. Human sacrifice was a diminishing practice but still occurring on many continents and slavery was generally regarded as normal. Massacres were not unusual and not always in battle. In 88BC King Mithridates of Pontus (Turkey) is reputed to have arranged the simultaneous massacre of every person of Roman and Italian origin or inclination living in Anatolia (Asian Turkey) – some 80,000 men, women and children plus their slaves in a single day. He didn't confine himself to Romans though, he is also recorded as having disposed of his mother, brother and almost any individual who threatened or upset him. Cruelty was unfortunately a characteristic of the Age and life was cheap.

If one includes Macedon in its immediate north, there can be few greater contributors to the advancement of western society than that of **Iron Age Greece**. Tribal groupings formed into city-states from around 800BC and, when not fighting each other, focused on relatively small-scale agriculture and trade. Athens to the south and Macedon to the north developed into major centres, with the former introducing a form of democracy and the latter becoming a militaristic monarchy. Under threat from Persia, King Philip II of Macedon sought by force and diplomacy to unite the Greek city-states, accomplishing this (with the exception of Sparta) in 337BC. Dying shortly thereafter it was left to his son Alexander the Great to bring Sparta into the fold and then invade Persia. Success there facilitated further expansion and Alexander soon invaded NW India and Pakistan, developing a major empire, including significant parts of Asia and Egypt.

Alexander's death in 323BC was succeeded by a series of civil wars which tore his empire apart. Greek power and influence gradually diminished over the remainder of the Age, although very evident still in Alexandria, possibly then the largest city in the world, which, though the Egyptian capital, was ruled by Ptolemies of Macedonian-Greek origin. Ultimately Greece fell under almost complete Roman domination after the battle of Corinth in 146BC. Greece's rich and ongoing legacy to the world was a wide range of advances in education, philosophy, arts, medicine, science, astronomy and architecture.

Of the many other notable developments of the Iron Age, perhaps the most profound was that of **Rome**. Founded around 750BC, Rome became a city-state, one of many such on the Italian peninsula. At a defensible site (and where there had been previous fortified settlements) and well situated, slightly inland on the River Tiber, the people prospered. Monarchies gave way to a form of republican rule with elected magistrates around 500BC and the city grew with developing trade, especially in salt, until sacked by a force of Celtic Gauls in 390BC. This may well have been a 'wake -up' call for the Romans, who afterwards improved their defences and became more militarily aggressive, such that within another hundred years they controlled over half the Italian peninsula.

Roman expansionism then became something of a way of life in the late Iron Age. Citizenship was highly prized, as was democratic governance, although her society was highly stratified, with status being more a function of wealth and ancestry than knowledge or ability (a situation notable in many modern societies). Her history in this period marked a rise from ashes to empire within the space of a few hundred years and no brief overview could hope to accord it proper justice. Suffice it to say that Rome in this Age was replete with a panoply of heroes and villains within a society marked by noble aspirations, widespread corruption, civil strife and an enduring faith in its own superiority. Her laws and mechanisms of government; the military might of her infantry Legions; and remarkable feats of engineering, together with extensive road and bridge building were enduring features. Within the span of this Age Rome also gave us the modern calendar of 365 days, the concept of a standing army and impressive examples of logistical achievement. Less attractive features included the slaughter of vast numbers of people or their sale into slavery and the wholesale plundering of the treasures of defeated and subordinate nations.

By the end of this Age (1BC), Rome dominated every land bordering the Mediterranean Sea, including the modern nations of Spain, Portugal, France, Italy, Yugoslavia, Albania, Greece, Bulgaria, Turkey, Syria, Lebanon, Israel, Egypt and northern Africa.

In the far east of the Asian continent, **China** had not, in this period being addressed, entered its own Iron Age and remained reliant upon bronze implements. A potentially stable rule under the Zhou dynasty had begun, which had replaced an oppressive Shang dynasty. Absolute dynastic rule prevailed, under a king who took on religious symbolism as "Son of Heaven", although both ancestor worship and polytheism were common. The south of the country was primarily agrarian whilst nomadic pastoralism typified the north. Around 770BC the latter tribes rebelled, attacked the capital, killing the king and introducing another period of internal instability which continued until around 221BC when the militaristic ruler of Qin State forced unification and assumed the title of Emperor. That period of instability did, however, see the emergence of a new scholarly social class who took on clerical, educational and administrative functions. One such man who rose to prominence and remains well regarded in modern times was K'ung Fu-tzu, or Confucius, who advocated social order and became renowned for his writings on philosophy.

Harsh measures enacted under Qin rule inevitably led to discontent and, ultimately, rebellion. In 202BC the king of the Han tribe defeated a competing rebel and became Emperor. China entered a period of improving prosperity and enlightened social measures under the Han Dynasty which continued throughout the remainder of this Age. Standard weights and measures were in place, the first national census had been undertaken and grain production increased, whilst Confucian philosophy had been adopted by the State. Unlike some other times and peoples, the Chinese hierarchy was then actively promoting talent and ability wherever it might be found.

By the end of the Iron Age our partly-wise forebears numbered some 200 – 300 million, although estimates vary widely.

IRON AGE – MILESTONES 1000BC – 1BC

10th CENTURY BC

Assyrian Empire begins 350-year hostile expansion from Mesopotamia; uses both infantry and war chariots.

King Solomon of Judea dies; kingdom splits into Israel to North and Judea to South. Egypt invades, Jerusalem plundered.

Trade-based Etruscan civilisation coalesces in towns in NW Italy.

9th CENTURY BC

Assyria defeats Babylonia, annexes Phoenicia (Syria/Lebanon), controls Eastern Mediterranean.

Carthage (Tunisia) founded by Phoenicians.

Rice emerges as major component of Chinese diet.

Widespread leather tanning evident.

8th CENTURY BC

Greek city-states begin emerging; first Olympic Games at Olympia (776BC).

Nomadic Xianyun tribes from NW Asian steppes invade and destroy Chinese Zhou capital; new Zhou regime move to Luoyang on Yellow River; Eastern Zhou period of over 500 years begins.

Indian "caste" system formalised.

Rome founded (legend of Romulus & Remus).

Assyria establishes a standing army; repeatedly invades different areas of the Levant.

The Iliad and Odyssey are documented (attributed to Homer).

Phoenician colonists settle in Spain, plant Olive trees.

China introduces crop rotation, grain storage for famine relief and rental system for farm equipment.

7th CENTURY BC

Greek population expands into other Mediterranean areas: cities being ruled by merchants ("tyrants") with slave labour: silver coinage introduced: Pythagoras runs school for medicine, mathematics, astronomy: land becoming devoid of trees due excessive harvesting.

Etruscan cities flourish in Italy; alphabet in use possible basis for Latin.

Assyria continues its warlike expansion; sacks Babylon, invades Egypt but suffers defeat by Medes (Iran) and begins decline with internal strife, collapsing as an empire in about 610BC.

6th CENTURY BC

Greek Anaximander produces first map of the known world

King Nebuchadnezzar II of Babylon destroys Jerusalem after repeated uprisings.

Confucius (Kung Fu-tse) advocates education and philosophy in China.

Persian empire is born (Iran) and embarks on massive war of conquest, annexing Assyria, Mesopotamia, Syria, Armenia, Cappadocia (Turkey), Babylonia and Egypt.

Buddhism begins in India under Siddhartha Gautama (Buddha).

Rome establishes itself as a republic with a form of representational democracy (509BC).

5th CENTURY BC

Roman republicans defeat attempt at restoration of monarchy by confederation of coastal towns ("Latin League") at Battle of Lake Regillus.

Ionian (W Turkey) Greeks, Athens and Cyprus revolt against Persian rule, beginning 20 years of war between Persia and Greece. Significant battles included Marathon (490BC), Thermopylae and Salamis (480BC) and Plataea (479BC).

Iron in common use in China, well after other developed countries.

Athens and Sparta in conflict (Peloponnesian War). Many innocents massacred.

Celts (Greek: *Keltoi*) colonise Britain from Central Europe.

Plague arises in Greece and Rome (Spartans kill all visitors).

Greek physician Hippocrates determines that diseases neither "spontaneous nor supernatural" in origin.

4th CENTURY BC

Wheat evident in Greece where city-states descend into chaos.

Magnificent tomb built for Mausolus, ruler of Halicarnassus, Ionian Greek city (now Turkey). Origin of term "mausoleum".

Large (18 metre) canoes evident in Scandinavia with iron weapons and crews of twenty.

Macedonia (N Greece) defeats Athenian and Theban forces, after which Alexander (the Great) becomes king, destroys Thebes, invades Asia Minor, Persia and India. Founds city of Alexandria (Egypt), destroys Persian capital (Persepolis), conquers Samarkand (C. Asia). Dies of fever in Babylon aged 33.

Rome takes most of this century to control Southern and central Italy, introduces pay for its army but suffers the sack of the city by Gauls who it 'buys off' (390BC). It establishes a treaty with Carthage.

Atomic theory proposed by the Ionian Greek philosopher Democritus.

China was experiencing violent internal feuding between regional lords rejecting Zhou rule and involving seven 'warring States'.

3rd CENTURY BC

Carthage (Tunisia) dominates trade in the Mediterranean, including slaves, ivory and skins.

Pharos Lighthouse constructed in Alexandria; lasts around 1,600 years. Greek head of Alexandrian library, Eratosthenes, calculates circumference of Earth to remarkable accuracy: appreciates that Earth is spherical, not flat.

Rome mints first silver coin (denarius). First Punic War begins (264BC) against Carthage over Sicily and lasts 23 years. Both sides suffer enormous losses but forces Rome to develop naval forces, building some 1,000 galleys over the course of the war. End result is Roman annexation of Sicily and discontent in Carthage.

The second Punic war erupts in 218BC and lasts 17 years. Notable for Carthaginian general Hannibal surprising Rome by marching overland through Spain and France over Alps into Italy. At the Battle of Cannae he defeated the largest ever Roman army, killing or capturing 120,000 soldiers. He was eventually defeated by Roman general Scipio who threatened Carthage itself in 201BC.

Qin leadership in China progressively annexes other "warring States" to assume China's first centralised power (221BC) and beginning 2,000 years of imperial rule. Construction of Great Wall of China commences. Qin defeated; Han Dynasty begins (202BC).

2nd CENTURY BC

Rome entered the century at war with Macedon which had been troubling Rome's allied Greek city-states. This occupied three years but ended with Rome having control of all Greece. Antiochus III, a Greek ruler of Syria and W Asia, a self-declared champion of Greek freedom, invaded in 192BC. He was defeated by Roman forces at Magnesia (Thessaly) in 190BC. All Syrian possessions in Europe/Asia ceded to Rome.

A third Punic war erupted (149BC) as a punitive expedition against Carthage (Tunis) on dubious grounds, fought entirely on Carthaginian territory and lasted three years. Ending in a successful assault on Carthage itself, the Romans sacked the city and took 50,000 prisoners who were sold into slavery.

Paved streets and first stone bridge appear in Rome.

Romans declare January 1 as first day of the year.

Gross mistreatment after Roman occupation generates two successive slave uprisings in Sicily with great loss of life before order is restored.

Judaea, under nominal control by Seleucid Empire (an offshoot of the Macedonian Empire), encounters uprising by Jewish rebels (Maccabees) intent on removing Greek influence. Military success against weak Seleucid response leads to semi-autonomous rule by "Hasmonean Dynasty" (from family name of rebel leader). Dynasty destroyed by client King Herod with Roman military support.

Chinese vessels visit E India.

Cimbri (Celtic/Germanic) tribes achieve major defeat of two Roman armies at battle of Arausio: over 100,000 Romans killed (105BC). Four years later Roman forces achieve an equally sizeable victory over the Cimbri (Raudine Plain, N Italy), virtually wiping them out.

1st CENTURY BC

Civil war arises in Italy between Rome Republic and regional tribal cities which demanded citizenship and voting rights. Three years of conflict ensued, ending through a combination of concessions, political manoeuvring and brute force by the Republic.

A third slave revolt erupts (73BC), this time on the mainland, led by a captive gladiator named Spartacus. Lasts two years until put down.

A period of Roman expansionism begins, initiating a transition from Republic to Empire.

- Subjugation of Judaea and Palestine by Pompey (64/63BC).
- Invasion of Gaul (58BC) and Britain (55BC) (Gaius Julius Caesar).
- Caesar recalled to face trial; crosses River Rubicon with Legion, starts civil war.
- Caesar defeats Pompey, becomes absolute Roman ruler (48BC).
- Caesar supports Queen Cleopatra in Egypt, moves to Asia Minor, defeats rebellious King of Pontus (Turkey).
- Caesar returns to Rome with Cleopatra, destroys 14-legion Republican army (46BC).
- Caesar declared dictator of Rome for life but is assassinated; Cleopatra returns to Egypt (44BC).
- Octavian (Caesar's adopted son) defeats Antony & Cleopatra who then suicide.

- Octavian assumes role of Emperor ["Princeps"] of Roman Empire (27BC).

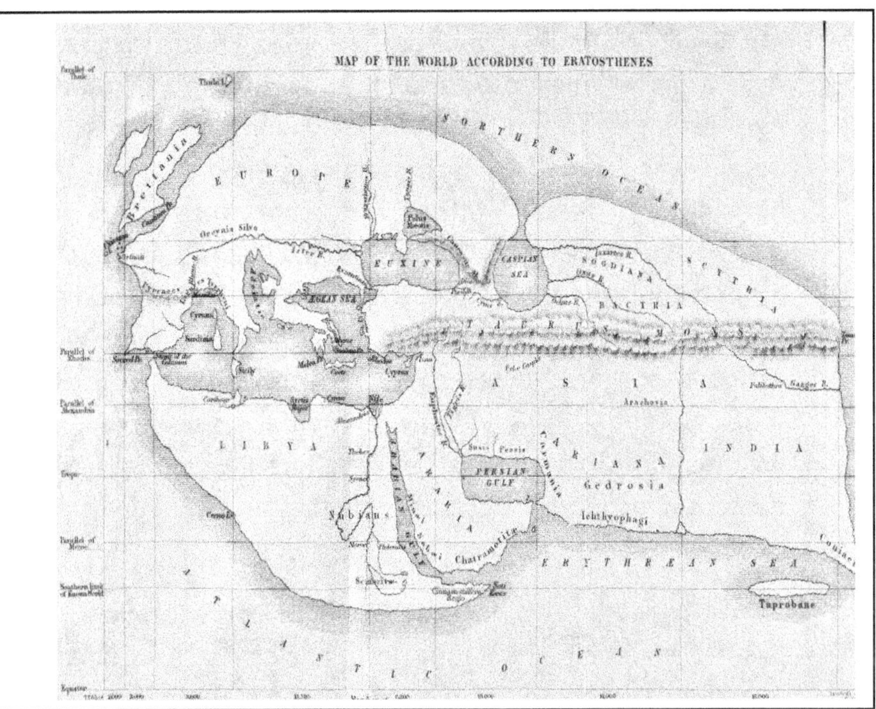

Fig 2: - Map of known world circa 194BC
(Reconstruction published in 1883 by Edward Bunbury of map by Eratosthenes of Alexandria courtesy Wikipedia)

THE MIGRATION AGE: 1-500

There is a part of our historical journey – a gap in the timeline of sorts – to which wiser persons seem to have avoided giving a title. This is the time between the end of the Iron Age (although that period could be extended to suit on a regional basis) and the beginning of either the Medieval or Middle Ages from the year 400 or the Dark Ages from 500. I choose to call that period the "Migration Age" extending from 1 to 500AD. With many exceptions the period was marked by wholesale migration plus one of humanity's least attractive characteristics: an overwhelming desire to have what they lacked and some other people had, whether that be power or resources (land, gold, silver etc). Migration in this period, as ever, was variously triggered by escape from conflict (and in these times potential slavery), environmental issues (crop or pasture decline, often due deteriorating rainfall), or perceived economic advantage (a better life). All three issues were at play during the Migration Age.

The Huns, a largely nomadic confederation of pastoralist peoples inhabiting north and central Asia, began migrating westwards during this period, with dramatic consequences on those already living on the steppes, especially north of the Black Sea. Though subsisting on cattle, sheep and goats, their principal animal was the horse and collectively they were excellent riders. They used that skill to devastating effect as horse archers, using a form of compound reflex bow and drove all opposing tribal groups before them. They gained a reputation for ruthless savagery and, having defeated the Sarmatians and Goths, amongst others, they turned their attention to the Roman Empire towards the end of the fourth century. A weakened Rome was forced to treat with them and the Huns occasionally became Roman mercenaries but also relied significantly on tribute and plunder, brooking no opposition. Their demise was achieved through an alliance of Roman and Visigoth forces in a battle in northern France ("Catalamian Plains") which involved heavy losses on both sides. Although the battle itself was inconclusive, the outcome destroyed the aura of invincibility of the Huns which dispersed only a few years later.

Before the advent of the Huns and at its very beginning, this period augured well for humanity's progress, at least in Europe and its immediate surrounds, as Pax Romana (Roman peace) prevailed, a period of enforced peace and stability within the **Roman empire**. The times were not actually peaceful, though, and the concept of that being a time of peace was largely a domestic propaganda exercise initiated by Emperor Augustus (Octavian) to enable good governance without resort to constant external wars. Harshly judgemental as it may seem, it is difficult to escape a conclusion that mankind made no, or at least very limited, progress immediately thereafter, largely thwarted by men and women determined to seek power for its own sake and regardless of the consequences. In this period preceding the demise of the western empire in 476 the people of Rome variously enjoyed or suffered under the rule of some ninety-two emperors. There was rarely any time in that period when the empire was not under some form of external threat or internal revolt.

The demise of the Roman empire, or to be more accurate the western component of that empire, cannot reasonably be laid at the door of any single cause or event. Rather, the causes were multiple and lay in a combination of internal weaknesses and increasing external pressures. By the fourth and fifth centuries, Rome was overpopulated and its government could not feed the people from its own resources, being heavily reliant on imports. This was manageable provided there was competent governance and no diminution in overseas supplies. Corruption, internal struggles for power and reduced crop availability because of variations in weather generated increasing difficulty. Equally, Rome had historically relied upon the strength of its armed forces both for protection and for the economic benefits overseas victories brought with them. The capability of the army and its reduced number of legions had been progressively diminished over many years just as the military abilities of potential adversaries (often Roman trained) were increasing. An occasionally raised, but often dismissed, factor was the introduction of Christianity. One draws a long bow to blame Christianity as such, but one cannot change a whole population's religious beliefs by edict, as Theodosius attempted in 380, without generating a degree of confusion and disaffection amongst the populace. The decline of empire was doubtless exacerbated by incompetent leadership but that was just one of the many factors involved.

In **China**, the beginning of this Age saw the re-emergence of the Han dynasty after the seizure of the imperial throne by a court official. Though that provided the prospect of peaceful development, the seeds of discontent were already sown, with landowner power and taxes increasing in equal proportion to the burden on peasants. Wealthier landowners recruited armies to protect their interests and impoverished peasants were inevitably attracted to rebel gangs. Confucianism seems to have waned as a central tenet of behaviour, whilst Daoism and Buddhism gained in popularity as social inequity grew. Warlords progressively divided the empire between themselves then disputed the agreed divisions such that, apart from brief periods of national unity, the country descended into chaos. This was especially so in the north where incursions by Mongolian tribes added to civil strife and banditry so that both order and the economy collapsed. Large scale internal migration from the north added to the political and economic pressures on areas further south. By the end of this period China was in something of a mess; its population in decline, no central authority and with a clear north-south divide within its borders. Oddly, perhaps, poetry and philosophy flourished, albeit sporadically. Perhaps China's greatest contribution to mankind's progress in this Age was the development in around 105 of a form of paper which could be produced economically and on a large scale, thus facilitating the much wider spread of knowledge.

India at the start of this period was something of an exception to the dynastic rule found elsewhere. The previous Mauryan empire had collapsed some two centuries previously, largely due to weak rule, and a large number of minor kingdoms prevailed. This changed in the mid third century when an empire founded by Sri Gupta arose and which encompassed most of India by the end of the period. Though achieved through conquest – some twenty-one separate kingdoms were claimed to have been overrun – the Gupta Empire was best known for its cultural and scientific developments. The empire enjoyed decentralised rule with policies favouring ethical behaviour and relied significantly on both agriculture and trade, notably in silk, ivory, leather and spices such as pepper, especially with Rome. The dynasty is claimed to be the origin of chess and was one of the first to recognise that the earth is both round and rotates upon its own axis. Despite having a large and well-developed military based upon armoured cavalry and horse archers, the dynasty was under increasing threat from Huns from the north toward the end of the period and began a gradual decline.

In the Americas another civilisation, that of the **Maya**, was approaching its zenith. Building progressively over some two thousand years, the Maya people had been carving an empire of city-states from the mountains and rainforest from south-east Mexico to Guatemala, including almost the entire Yucatan Peninsula. There was an extensive internal trade network, although no evidence of external trading and the currency was based upon the Cocoa bean. The Maya built in stone, with some forty cities, some with a population of around 100,000. Their religion was formal with a hierarchy of priests and a diverse range of gods: there is evidence of ritual human sacrifice. Food sources were relatively basic, mainly comprising corn, squash and beans. In many ways, though, the Maya were a highly sophisticated people: they developed complex hieroglyphic writing, recorded their history with detailed calendars and were one of, if not the, first people to identify a zero in their mathematics. This was the "classic" period of Mayan culture although the city-states were still constantly warring with each other. The Maya later became particularly noted for their intricate "Long Count" calendar which generated much superstitious alarm when it neared its end in December 2012.

The movement of people in this Age was not confined to wholesale forays such as by the Huns and Goths, but also by smaller groups and individuals in the pursuit of trade. Perhaps the best-known example is the Silk Road between China and Eastern Europe but there were others and this ongoing movement of people fostered both trade and the expansion of knowledge. What also developed were minor empires: two examples of which in Africa were **Axum** (Ethiopia/Somalia) and **Ghana** (Mauritius/Senegal/Mali). Axum, sited at the southern end of the Red Sea, flourished in this period with a basis in agriculture but extensively involved in trade with Egypt, Arabia and India, especially in gold and ivory. The local civilisation was advanced with multi-storey stone buildings, its own coinage and script and it expanded to cover much of the north-east African coast after a successful conflict with the kingdom of Kush in the mid-fourth century. The empire of Ghana (not the modern-day Ghana) covered what is now Mauritania, Senegal and Mali and became a feudal kingdom with a significant population of around 20,000. Wealth there came primarily from trade in gold, of which it was a rich source, plus ivory and salt. That trade flourished in the third century with the advent of the camel which facilitated movement across the Sahara Desert. This empire was destined to last around a thousand years.

By the end of this period (500AD) Earth's population had reached around 200 million.

MIGRATION AGE – MILESTONES 1-500

1ST CENTURY

1 - Notional year of birth of Jesus of Nazareth – (no year zero in Gregorian calendar and calendar revisions put birth at 4BC).
Japan first cultivates rice from imports from China.
9 -Some 20,000 Roman legionaries killed by Germanic tribes at Teutoburg Forest.
China introduces 10% tax on professionals and skilled labourers.
20 - Evidence of bronze shields in Britain.
25 - Eastern Han dynasty founded in China; 500-year domination of Vietnam begins.
26 - Pontius Pilate begins 10-year rule as Procurator [chief financial officer/ governor] of Judea.
33 - Pontius Pilate has Jesus of Nazareth crucified for sedition.
38 - Roman Governor of Egypt (Flaccus) orders Jews of Alexandria into smaller city area - this becomes the first 'ghetto'.
43 - Emperor Claudius leads expedition to conquer Britain. A legate Vespasian comes to the fore with a succession of victories over British tribes.
44 - Jesus' apostle James who preached the former's divinity is executed.
48 - Roman legions invade Wales.
61 - British tribe Iceni led by Queen Boudica (Boadicea) and Trinovantes revolt against Roman rule and sack London; revolt crushed by Romans, Boudica dies.
62 - Earthquake (5 February) severely damages Pompeii.

64 - Fire destroys most of Rome which is then progressively rebuilt.

66 - Jews in Galilee and Judaea rebel against Roman rule. Vespasian tasked with its suppression and is largely successful when Emperor Nero suicides, plunging Rome into chaos and civil war between claimants to the succession. Eventually Vespasian garners enough support from the legions to return to Rome as Emperor (70).

70 - Christian gospel of Mark written about this time.

79 - Mount Vesuvius erupts (24 August) devastating Pompeii & Herculaneum.

98 - Trajan becomes Roman Emperor.

Malaria and Anthrax evident in rural Rome about this time.

2nd CENTURY

105 - China begins use of an improved form of paper made from bark and hemp waste (earlier versions dating back some 200 years) differing from papyrus in use in Egypt and Rome.

Dacia (Romania), Armenia, Assyria and Mesopotamia (later abandoned) progressively dominated by Rome.

115 - Jewish uprisings in Cyrenaica (Libya), Cyprus, Judea, Mesopotamia and Egypt ("Kitos War") involving widespread massacres of Greeks and Romans, virtually depopulating some areas of Middle East.

117 - Rome suppresses Jewish uprisings. Jews forbidden from Cyprus.

124 - Palace eunuchs seize power in China, put 10-year-old on throne.

125 - Plague and famine sweep N Africa.

132 - Further Jewish revolt in Judea ("Bar Kokhba Revolt") lasting over two years: finally suppressed by Rome.

135 - Jews (including Christian Jews) barred from Jerusalem.

161 - First Roman emissary visits China via Vietnam.

165 - Antonine Plague (probably Smallpox) decimates Roman Empire over fifteen-year period and also apparent in China.

184 – Daoist religious in China launch rebellion; eunuchs massacred, warlords and nobles divide empire between them.

3rd CENTURY

200 - Romans construct defensive wall around London 6 metres high and 3.2km long.

212 - Roman Emperor Caracalla extends citizenship to all free inhabitants of the Empire (some 30M+ people).

224 - Battle of Hormozdgan (Iran) sees Parthian (or Arsacid) empire defeated by Sasanian (Persian) forces. This marks the beginning of the Neo-Persian Empire stretching from Eastern Mediterranean, Iran, Iraq, Pakistan and parts of southern Arabia to central Asia.

250 - Gunpowder invented in China.

255 - Plague evident throughout Egypt and Europe.

256 - Brief (60-year) period of unity in China under Jin dynasty.

260 - Battle of Edessa (Turkey) sees major defeat of Roman army by Sasanian forces - some 16,000 Romans killed or captured.

270 - A short-lived empire arises, led by Queen Zenobia of Palmyra, controlling Rome's eastern provinces (Syria, Palestine, Egypt, Asia west of Persia). Zenobia asserts independence while Rome is distracted by Gothic invasion but ultimately defeated (**272**).

274 - Seagoing (30 metre) oar-powered vessels constructed in Japan.

282 - Having endured almost fifty years of attacks by Alemanni, Goths and Franks, Roman forces drive those Germanic tribes from Gaul.

4th CENTURY

304 - Period of "Sixteen Kingdoms" begins in China with civil war and chaos prevailing for over 100 years.

311 – Xiongnu, a nomadic confederation of tribes based in Mongolia sack the city of Luoyang (NE China) killing some 30,000 people.

313 – Roman Constantine accepts Christianity.

317 – China divides into Northern and Southern dynasties.

319 – Chandragupta becomes king of Gupta Empire which rules much of northern India.

330 – Emperor Constantine renames city of Byzantium as Constantinople which is declared new capital of Roman Empire and destined to become largest and wealthiest city in Europe.

350 – Roman Empire under increasing threat from Alemanni, Huns, Picts, Persians and Goths.

378 – Goths achieve major defeat of Roman forces at Battle of Adrianople (NW Turkey) killing over 10,000.

380 – Christianity is declared the state religion of Roman Empire by Edict of Thessalonica by Emperor Theodosius I.

391 – Emperor Theodosius demands that all non-Christian works be destroyed.

5th CENTURY

401 – Visigoths (Western Goths) invade northern Italy; halted at Battle of Pollentia (Pollenzo, N Italy) in 402.

406 – Vandals, a Germanic tribe originally from central Europe, invade northern Gaul.

408 – Visigoths lay siege to Rome; exact tribute and leave but return two years later and sack and plunder the city.

410 – Last Roman troops leave Britain, too late to stop the sack of Rome. Goths withdraw but re-establish themselves in Gaul and Spain.

428 – Vandals, displaced from Spain, invade north Africa in large numbers.

434 – Attila becomes co-leader of the Huns and leads wide-ranging incursions into Roman territories.

439 – Vandals seize Carthage (N Tunisia), establish it as their capital.

441 – Angles and Saxons begin settling in SE Britain, destroying Roman towns.

451 – Council of Chalcedon (Kadikoy, Turkey), a large convocation of Christian Bishops, approves "Nicene Creed" and declares Bishop of "New Rome" (Constantinople) as having same status as Bishop of "Old Rome".

453 – Attila the Hun dies after withdrawing from a successful campaign in Italy.

455 – Vandal force attacks Rome from seaward and sacks the city.

476 - Germanic Flavius Odoacer (Odovacar) deposes Roman emperor and becomes king of Italy with support of his Rigii, Heruli and Scirii soldiers. This effectively ends the western Roman empire although eastern empire prevails, becoming known as Byzantine Empire, based on Constantinople.

486 – Franks (Clovis I) defeat Roman forces in Gaul and establish Merovingian Dynasty.

489 – Ostrogoth (eastern Goth) Theodoric, supported by Eastern Emperor Zeno, invades Italy, murders Odoacer and establishes Ostrogoth kingdom of Italy – for all practical purposes a new western Roman empire.

495 – Chinese Weis dynasty establishes Luoyang (central China) as capital.

495 – Kingdom of Wessex established in Britain.

Fig 3: - Tribal peoples' movements into Roman Empire 1-500AD

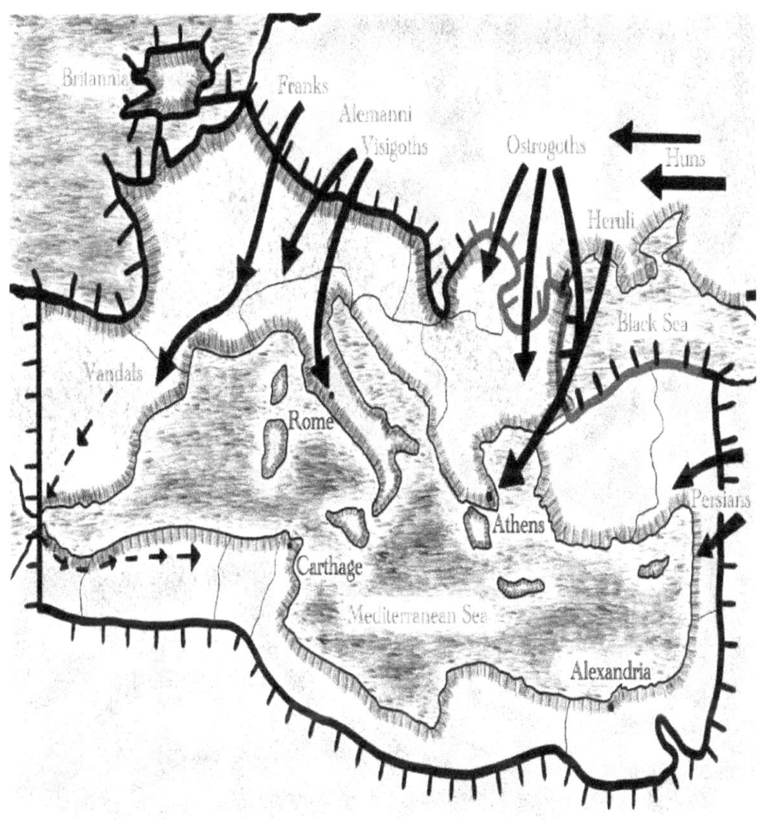

Fig 4: - Tribal peoples' movements into Britain 1-500AD

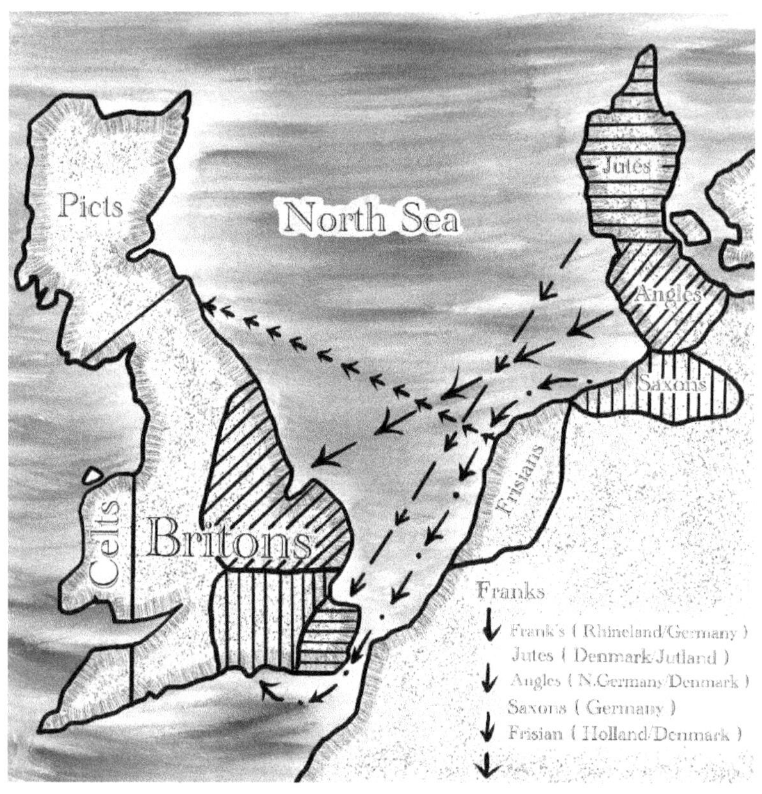

THE DARK AGE: 500-1,000AD

This period, for only partly-wise reasons, is rounded to between 500 and 1,000AD and was not "dark" in any literal sense – the sun still shone as usual and, overall, it was really no more violent a time than many others. Coined by an Italian in the 14th Century, the term related originally to his chagrin at the ongoing absence of classic Latin literature. The period is often referred to as the Dark Ages (plural) and history is certainly full of those, but since we are addressing only one Age allotted this formal title, for our partly-wise purposes it is the Dark Age (singular)!

Before reviewing the key developments of this part of our journey it is perhaps timely to contemplate the environment of the ordinary person then living. With a population but a fraction of that of modern times, that environment was largely marked by peace and quiet, without the bustle of modernity; little or no mechanical background noise nor related fumes. Word of mouth was the prevailing source of news from outside the immediate surrounds. Family was the prevailing core of society although the life of women would have been quite subordinate and vulnerable to predation. There were no prisons so justice tended to be arbitrary and extreme. Superstition was generally deep and widespread, as was slavery, although the latter varied in the degree of degradation involved, occasionally being entered into voluntarily for the benefits of food and shelter. Physical strength would have been highly valued but life itself was fragile. Poor hygiene, infrequent washing and no established system of health or welfare support and rudimentary medical knowledge would have made illness an often-fatal occurrence.

It is thus unsurprising that a pandemic would then have had devastating consequences and that was certainly the case with the "**Plague of Justinian**". So named after Justinian, then Emperor of the East, this was a form of Bubonic plague now known to be spread from infected fleas commonly found on rats. Known for its symptom of swollen lymph nodes ("buboes"), those infected become very ill and with a high, often fifty percent, rate of mortality. First recorded around 541, the plague began somewhere in northern Africa and spread throughout the Sasanian (Persian) and east Roman empires then west to Greece, Italy and Britain causing the loss of up to fifty million lives, whether directly or indirectly through starvation. The plague would see a repeat presence over the next few centuries.

In **Britain** the populace was entering a turbulent time with an influx of immigrants from the continent which began toward the end of the Migration Age. Initially invited to assist incursions by the Picts, the arriving Saxons had found a land denuded of military protection after the Roman withdrawal and with a total population little more than that currently found on much smaller islands such as Cyprus or Fiji. Joined by other Germanic tribal groups, notably Angles, Jutes and others they had established settlements in the south (mainly Saxon) and east (mainly Angle) by the beginning of the Dark Age. Numbers of immigrants increased significantly over the next few centuries and the native Britons were either pushed westwards by force of arms, killed or in most cases simply assimilated. As settlements grew, hierarchies developed and a series of minor kingdoms arose, most notably those of Wessex, Mercia and Kent.

Christianity spread widely amongst the Anglo-Saxons after the arrival of the monk Augustine in 597 and conversion of Aethelberht (Ethelbert), king of Kent, then a dominant kingdom. Despite ongoing rivalry between the various kingdoms, very often involving violent conflict, Christianity flourished, as did the church itself which progressively accumulated land and great wealth. This eventually attracted the interest of Scandinavian raiders (**Vikings**) who in 793 outraged Christendom by sacking the monastery of Lindisfarne in Northumbria. With little by way of organized Anglo-Saxon defence, the Viking raids then became more extensive and by 850 they were wintering in locally conquered territory. Within a few decades the Viking strategy had changed from plunder to conquest and residence, such that they held sway over large parts of northern and eastern Britain. It was not until 878 that the tide turned when Alfred ("the Great") who had assumed the role of King of the Anglo-Saxons, achieved a significant victory over a Viking force at the Battle of Edington (Wiltshire). It would be left to his successors, including his heroic and redoubtable daughter Aethelflaed, to finally halt Viking incursions at the Battle of Tettenhall (west Midlands) in 910.

In the **mid-East and Mediterranean** region, trouble was brewing. A dispute between the Islamists of Medina and a Jewish enclave further east which was accused of plotting to attack Medina and/or assassinate Muhammad resulted in a pre-emptive attack on those Jews in 628. The success of that attack and consequent status and demonstration of power impressed the area Bedouin who promptly vowed allegiance and converted to Islam. Muhammad's principles were broadly attractive, including rights for women, care for the plight of the poor and rejection of aristocratic privilege. By the time of the death of Muhammad four years later almost the whole of the Arabian Peninsula was in Muslim hands.

Mohammad's successors (caliphs) embarked almost immediately upon a program of rapid Islamic conquest. In a period when both the Sassanid and Byzantine empires were weakened from continual conflict, Muslim (Islamic) forces achieved considerable success, conquering Syria, Palestine, Egypt and Libya and completely subjugating the already disintegrating Sassanid (Persian) empire. Except in Arabia, where Muhammad had decreed that no two religions might dwell together, the conquerors did not initially impose their religion on subjugated Christians or Jews and religious pluralism was tolerated. Internal Muslim conflict did arise, however, and in 681 a battle arose between those who believed the religious leader should be elected (Sunni) and those who believed he should be descended from Muhammad (Shia). That schism, like the Christian division between Roman and Eastern (Greek) orthodoxies, has never been satisfactorily resolved.

Regardless of such internal conflicts, by 750 the Muslim caliphate had encompassed Spain, North Africa,

Egypt, Arabia, the Levant, Persia and as far north as the Caucasus Mountains. This constituted a 'golden age' of Islamic civilization with art, literature and science all flourishing. Thereafter the empire began to fragment with varying sects forming and seizing control of their individual domains and forming independent emirates.

The Dark Age in **China** opened after widespread chaos and upheaval. In the north the capital Luoyang was developed over seven years into a grand city of monasteries, palaces and all the machinery and infrastructure of government and then simply abandoned. In the south there began a degree of stability after a period of incompetent rule and many coups with the accession of the Liang dynasty in 502. North and south, however remained intractably opposed. A more determined ruler came to power in the north in 581, amassed a sizeable force and invaded the south, ultimately achieving his objective of reunifying the country in 589. Stability did not prevail for long. Punitive taxes and continued forced labour led to discontent amongst the peasantry; rebellion arose and the emperor was assassinated. A militant provincial governor then assumed power and began the Tang dynasty. That dynasty, which was to last almost three hundred years and though marked by innumerable inter-family killings to determine who should rule, proved stabilizing and efficient. Land reform, a trained bureaucracy, codified laws and state control of key industries such a salt, transport, mining and silk production all benefited growth and prosperity.

A notable aspect of this period in China, just as in Britain with Aethelflaed, was the rise to prominence of powerful women. The daughter of the dynastic founder, one Princess Pingyang, was as militaristic as her father and personally led her own forces into battle. Later, and following a more devious route to power, arose Empress Wu Zetian, the only known ruling empress in China's history. She ruled independently between 690 and 705 but held the reins of power from well before that time and maintained her position with ruthless efficiency. Her son replaced her on the throne after a palace coup but he in turn was poisoned by his wife and a series of relatively ineffective rulers then saw the decline of the Tang dynasty.

Internal feuding and open warfare saw China once again divided both into northern and southern areas of influence and within those areas as individual warlords sought power. The dying years of the Age saw the empire still riven by conflict but hope arose with the appointment (by his own troops) of a successful military commander as Emperor Taizu. He only ruled for sixteen years but brought peace and unification to a country desperately in need of exactly that.

Elsewhere in the world, a partly-wise summation of Dark Age progress would see much use of the word "decline". In **India** the Gupta empire ultimately collapsed in 543 after a combination of internal disputes over succession and external military threats: a somewhat common theme in the decline of empires. The invading Huns had managed to force their way into central India as early as 510 and the weakness of the central government, deprived of tax revenue by a series of feudal chieftains declaring independence, could do little to counter them.

Amongst the general population there was no great sense of loyalty to any central authority and the country gradually drifted into a patchwork of petty kingdoms. A similar condition was evident in the central American **Maya** civilization where there were systemic problems in governance such as lack of central control over trade and food distribution. Over a single century most cities, already overpopulated, had been abandoned and continuing warfare between those remaining favored retreat into walled mountain locations. Whilst drought may also have been a factor, by the end of the Age, the Maya civilization was well into terminal decline.

On the west coast of **South America** two other city-state civilizations had arisen and fallen. These were Huari (Wari) and Tiahuanaco (Tiwanaku) separate but similar very large settlements high in the Andes: the former in what is now Peru and the latter in Bolivia. Though these locations were probably occupied in far more ancient times, the people of this Age were evidently skilled in road building and large, sometimes massive, decorated stone structures and with societies sufficiently developed to have artisans producing jewelry, pottery and textiles. What may have generated their demise is speculative, possibly through extended drought, but these populations were dispersed by the end of the Age. Their genetic make-up is reportedly still evident in the modern populations of Peru and Bolivia respectively.

As the Dark Age closed in 1,000AD, Earth's population stood at around 300 million.

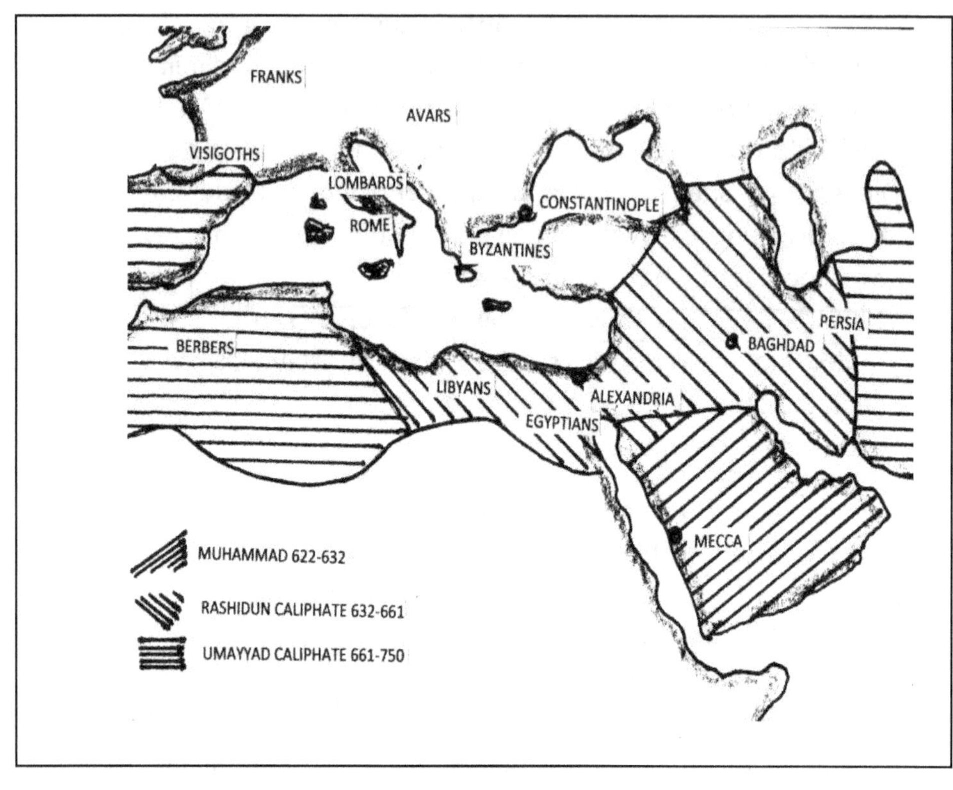

Fig 5: Islamic conquests in the Dark Age

THE DARK AGE – MILESTONES 500 - 1000

6TH CENTURY

502 - Liang Dynasty founded in China by a Buddhist scholar adopting the name Liang Wudi who marches on Nanking, causing large loss of life before that city fell.

532 – Ongoing conflict between Roman (Byzantine) and Persian forces halted with "Treaty of Perpetual Peace" – which actually lasted only eight years until 540.

541 – Great Plague of Justinian spreads throughout Mediterranean area, Northern Europe and Near East causing disruption, starvation and many deaths. Believed to have started in northern Africa, the pandemic was a form of bubonic plague with a death rate approaching 20 percent of any affected population. The plague reached Britain around 547 and was followed by multiple "waves" of plague over the following two centuries.

552 - Justinian sends Christian missionaries to China to smuggle out silkworms.

569 - Prophet Muhammad is born.

581 - Sui Dynasty (Emperor Wendi) comes to power, re-unifies China.

7th CENTURY

622 – Prophet Muhammad flees from Mecca to Medina; returns six years later and takes Mecca, issues explanation of Muslim faith. Qur'an (Koran), which becomes basis for Islamic religion, law, culture and politics, starts to be compiled. Major Islamic expansion by conquest begins.

651 – Islamic Caliphate conquers Sasanian Empire (last great Persian dynasty).

661 - Caliph Ali, cousin and son-in-law of Muhammad, is assassinated. Followers become known as Shiites (Shi'a). Islamic Umayyad Caliphate begins; becomes largest contemporary empire by its end in 750.

672 – Byzantines begin using "Greek Fire", an incendiary liquid, against Islamic forces, especially warships, with good success. The substance, probably launched using siphons or thrown in jars, is credited with saving Constantinople in the siege of 678.

682 - Islamic forces complete their conquest of north Africa including Tripoli, Tangiers, Carthage.

8TH CENTURY

708 - Tea becomes popular in China (safer than un-boiled water).

732 – Islamic forces of Umayyad Caliphate defeated by Franks at Battle of Tours (Aquitaine, France), halting their further progress.

750 – Islamic Umayyad caliphate falls; replaced by Abbasid Caliphate which is destined to last some 500 years.

751 - Muslim paper factory established at Samarkand using information from Chinese prisoners.

787 - Minor Viking (Scandinavian) raids on Britain begin (Wessex).

793 - Significant Viking raid on the monastery at the island of Lindisfarne (Northumbria) which is sacked and monks killed or enslaved. This strikes at the heart of Anglo-Saxon Christendom to great general British alarm.

795 - Viking attacks extend to Iona (Scotland) and Wales.

9TH CENTURY

800 - Charlemagne crowned Emperor of the Romans (western empire) having been king of the Franks since 768 and king of the Lombards since 774. This unification of central and northern Europe later became known as the Carolingian empire.

814 - Charlemagne dies. His son Louis "the Pious" assumes control of the empire but is plagued by civil wars, mainly fomented by his family, until his death in 840. Another brief civil war followed resulting in Francia being split into East and West – the former being the basis for modern Germany and the latter modern France. The Carolingian empire was effectively dissolved.

845 - Viking raids escalate throughout Europe with attacks spanning Britain, Ireland, France, Spain and the Mediterranean and as far inland as Novgorod (Russia). The size of raids also increased, attacking fleets sometimes numbering hundreds of longships.

871 - Alfred ("the Great") inherits kingdom of the West Saxons.

886 - Alfred becomes king of the Anglo Saxons. He spends the rest of his reign fighting Viking raids with mixed success until his death in 899.

10TH CENTURY

911 - Battle of Chartres (France) sees Viking jarl Rollo defeated by forces of King Charles ("the Simple"). Rollo agrees to baptism and defence of the Seine against further Viking raids in exchange for peaceful settlement. Area controlled by "Nortmanni" (Latin "Northmen") becomes Normandy.

930 - Viking settlers in Iceland form an "Althing" open-air assembly for elements of governance: possibly the world's first parliament.

1000 – Leif Erikson, a Norse explorer from Iceland, reputed to be the first European to land in North America (Newfoundland) which he calls Vinland. He establishes a brief settlement and returns to Iceland with timber and grapes.

MEDIEVAL (MIDDLE) AGE: 1000-1500

Europe in the Medieval Age was nothing short of being a tangled web of internal quarrelling and competing political ambition. Feudalism was the prevailing social system, by which is meant the exchange of labour for the provision of land and protection by some form of overlord. Ultimate power, notionally at least, was exercised by the emperor of the Roman Empire of the West, who, after 1254, became the Holy Roman Emperor. That empire was the dominant power in Europe at the time but was rarely stable and the addition of the title "Holy" gives some indication of the accompanying power of the Christian church and its leader in the west, the Pope. Christianity was widespread in Europe and very early in this period the church was flexing its muscles. In 1027 a "truce of God" was enacted which prohibited fighting on certain days and was later extended by a "peace of God" exempting clergy, women, children and peasants from attack under pain of religious sanction. Such sanctions were potentially serious as excommunication, for example, could relieve a soldier or serf from any service or responsibility to their lord.

Despite ongoing conflicts between Emperor and Pope; between feuding Germanic princes; between Christian Spaniards and Moors; between the Emperor and Italian Lombards; between England and France; and even between competing Popes; Europe in the early medieval period saw significant growth in both population and productivity. At least in part this may have been aided by a temporary warming of the northern European climate between the start of the period and about 1300, although improved agricultural practices such as the invention and use of the "heavy plough (plow)" which occurred in Europe about this time were probably more significant. Towns and communes flourished as did art and literature, together with the development of ocean-going vessels that enabled increased trade and exploration.

There are whole libraries of works by Wiser Persons devoted to this period in Europe. For our partly-wise purposes, though, it may be appropriate to simply highlight a few of the many significant events.

- **Norman Conquest of England**. Like much of the conflict elsewhere in Europe, the Norman invasion of England arose from a disputed claim to inheritance. The Anglo-Saxon King Edward (the Confessor) died childless and his brother-in-law Harold Godwinson succeeded him. William (the Conqueror) of Normandy, a first-cousin once-removed to Edward, contested Harold's right to succession and invaded with a substantial force. Unfortunately for Harold, a separate prior Norwegian invasion had occurred in the north of the country. Although successful in repelling the Norwegians on 25 September 1066, Harold was then around nine-days' march from Sussex where William landed three days later. Harold marched south but was defeated at Hastings and William was ultimately crowned on Christmas Day that year. The English nobility submitted or were killed but resistance continued for about five years. Much discontent arose due the confiscation of land, duly awarded to Norman followers, and similarly due to replacement of senior English clergy and officials with Normans and use of Norman French by officialdom, although formal documents remained in Latin. One particularly beneficial outcome was that slavery – and some ten percent of the English population were then slaves – was frowned upon and suppressed insofar as they could no longer be sold overseas.

- **The Crusades**. In 1095 the Byzantine emperor Alexius, concerned at an increasing threat from the Sunni Muslims of the Seljuk Turk empire, requested military support from the Pope. Seen favorably as an opportunity to wrest control of the Holy Land, and Jerusalem in particular, from Islamic control, what eventuated was a series of religious "crusades". European support for these crusades was partly religious, including prospective remission of sins; partly mercenary with the prospect of plunder; and partly as a rising tide of militaristic sentiment needed an outlet. If one dismisses an initial and amateurish "people's crusade", which was a disaster, the first crusade from 1096 met with good military success. Antioch was captured fairly quickly and Jerusalem fell after an extended siege in 1099. Regrettably the Muslim and Jewish citizens of the city were slaughtered in the process, including women and children. Strategically, one might well consider the crusade an unmitigated disaster, providing a focal point for centuries to come for otherwise peaceful and tolerant Muslims to remain uncompromisingly hostile to Christianity.

The second crusade came up against a competent general who had assumed the position of Sultan of Egypt – one Salah ad-Din, known to west as Saladin. He resoundingly defeated the crusader forces at the Battle of Hattin (near Tiberius, modern Israel) in 1187 and regained Jerusalem and most of the crusader cities. Six subsequent crusades had individually mixed success, though ultimately all failed and one in 1204 was notorious for sacking and pillaging Constantinople which had a longer-term effect in accelerating the fall of the Byzantine empire. A sixth crusade had perhaps the most success, more by diplomatic than military means, when the Holy Roman Emperor Frederick II negotiated a peace treaty that gave Christians access to Jerusalem and the port city of Acre. His efforts were negated when the Pope attacked his Italian holdings and he was forced to retire to defend them. The final straw in the collapse of any semblance of Christian power in the Levant occurred in 1244 when an allied force from Jerusalem, mainly crusaders, confronted an Islamic force of the Egyptian Sultan at the Battle of La Forbie near Gaza City (Palestine). The Christian force was thoroughly defeated and over five thousand crusaders died.

- **The Black Death**. The bubonic plague had previously struck Europe, but in 1348 it returned with a vengeance. Determination of its origin is speculative but we do know that over a two-year period it decimated the populations of West Asia, North

Africa, Sicily, Italy, Spain, France, England and Norway. With mortality being in the order of fifty percent, something like a third of Europe's population died, putting this plague as the most fatal in history. Although poor general hygiene certainly contributed, the rapid spread and high mortality do lead to a supposition that pneumonic plague rather than, or additional, to bubonic plague was involved. The significance of that being that airborne (not necessarily contact) transmission would also occur. With no identified cause and no cure, superstitions abounded and Jews were occasionally blamed and promptly massacred. One enlightened port city, Raguso (Croatia) did realize that the movement of people and cargo played a part so placed a thirty, then forty-day, hold on visitors or goods entering the city. That forty number (Latin *quadraginta*; Italian *quarant*) was the origin of the English word *quarantine.*

- **Hundred-Years War.** Advocates of hereditary monarchy could do well to study this dramatic period as an example of what can happen when things don't go to plan. In 1328 Charles IV of France died without male heir and under old Frankish law females such as his daughter could not inherit. The closest male relative was his nephew King Edward II of England who claimed the title. This was not acceptable to the French nobility who insisted on a native-born Frenchman as their king. They appointed Philip, Charles' cousin. Edward initially acceded to this situation until Philip decided that Gascony (SW France), which had historically been held by Edward's forebears, should be returned to direct French rule. Edward renewed his claim to the French throne, to be pursued by force. The ensuing war, fueled by nationalistic fervor, continued, albeit with long breaks and inhibited by the plague, for one hundred and sixteen years with an unsurprisingly large loss of life and property. England achieved early successes, especially by use of longbowmen versus cavalry, and notably at Crecy (1346) and Poitiers (1356). A treaty in 1360 temporarily halted direct hostilities, although French forces then gradually retook their lost possessions. Henry V of England revived the conflict in 1415 and had almost immediate success against a larger French army at Agincourt. He then lost any claim to honour or chivalry by ordering all the French prisoners killed. Both Henry V and Charles VI died in 1422. Whether inspired by Joan of Arc (captured and cruelly burned at the stake at age nineteen) or simply through better leadership, France subsequently had a succession of victories over English forces. They had achieved almost a complete victory except for Calais by 1453 and England later also lost that in 1558.

- **Wars of the Roses.** Civil war erupted in England in 1455 between rival claimants to the throne – the houses of Lancaster (symbolized by a red rose) and York (symbolized by a white rose). The causes and internal shifts of allegiance were complex and had little impact on the rest of Europe so are not further considered. Suffice it to say that the male line of both houses was extinguished in the process. Ultimately Henry Tudor returned from exile with

Lancastrian support and took the throne in 1485 as Henry VII, marrying Elizabeth of York to link both houses.

- **Renaissance.** Wiser Persons might place the Renaissance as a period or Age in its own right. It is, however a fairly woolly concept with indeterminate start and finish dates and related specifically to Europe, so is addressed here. The origin of the term is the Italian word *"rinascita"*, or "rebirth", used by the Italian artist Vasari in 1550 in writing about the arts having fallen into decay and needing a rebirth. Translated via the French to "renaissance", the term came to refer to a whole period of history some three hundred years later. Perhaps triggered by Greeks escaping the fall of Constantinople, there was certainly a revived Italian interest in classical antiquity which spread through Europe as a humanist focus on its five elements of poetry, grammar, history, philosophy and rhetoric. Realism and emotion became important in art and literature, whilst the era also saw a shift away from feudalism.

To the East the **Byzantine Empire**, more particularly the capital Constantinople itself, was enjoying some mixed blessings. Holdings in Italy were under threat from the Normans but the Bulgarian threat had been defeated. Overall, the empire stretched from the Danube River in the north to Crete in the south and between the Straits of Messina in the west to the Euphrates River (Iraq) in the east. Trade continued to flourish, even with Venice and Genoa, urban settlements were expanding, as was agricultural production, and the city itself was a leader in size, wealth and culture. Religious tensions remained, and came to a head in 1054 when a papal envoy entered the Hagia Sophia and formally excommunicated the Patriarch, thus effectively finalizing the split between the eastern and western Christian churches. Matters took something of a downward turn thereafter, exacerbated by Emperor Constantine IX demobilizing the core of the army. His timing was not astute, as the Muslim Seljuk Turks were continuing their westward expansion such that, by 1081, they occupied all of Anatolia (Turkey) – just a few hundred metres across the Bosporus at the entrance to the Black Sea.

Over the next four centuries the Byzantine Empire found itself assailed on all fronts. Much fought over, Anatolia descended into a patchwork of independent tribal groups until Osman I, a clan leader of uncertain origin, began achieving success against Byzantine forces and grew in stature. By 1400 his forces, known to the west as Ottoman Turks, had captured Adrianople (Edirne), the second largest Byzantine city, and most of Serbia and Bulgaria. They suffered a major set-back when defeated by a Mongol incursion in 1402 but recovered and were soon threatening all European trade with the east. In 1453 they conquered Constantinople itself and the Byzantine empire was at an end. The Islamic Ottoman empire was now established.

Of all the conflicts and developments in the Medieval Age, perhaps the most dramatic and of longest-lasting consequence was the advent of the **Mongols**. After a tribal chieftain's son called Temujin was declared universal leader of the Mongol tribes in 1206 and became known as **Genghis Khan**, there began one of the world's fastest, most widespread and ruthless series of conquests ever recorded. Excellent horse warriors, both male and female, the Mongols were highly mobile and equipped primarily with both compound bows and curved sabres together with siege engines gained through conflict with their Chinese neighbours. Supposedly triggered by confiscation of a Mogul caravan and accompanying ambassador, Genghis Khan's forces swept westwards in 1218 through Asia, massacring entire populations of any settlement or town that offered opposition. Within a single decade they had conquered the whole of central Asia, including Turkmenistan and Uzbekistan, Persia, parts of Russia to the north-west and as far east as the Korean border. The network of trade routes between China and Europe known as the Silk Road continued to flourish under the rule of Genghis, however, and authorized traders were accorded special protection.

The death of Genghis in 1227 caused only a temporary lull in the Mongol onslaught and his appointed successor Ogedei Khan successfully renewed assaults on Russia, Ukraine, Belarus, Persia, Georgia and Armenia. By 1240 when Ogedei died a Mongol army, one of many, was positioning to attack Vienna and the whole of Europe was under threat. Ogedei's death, however, triggered rivalry in selection of a new Great Khan and Mongol expansionism entered a holding pattern for some years except for ongoing attempts to defeat the Song Chinese. In the middle east, expansion into the Levant was stopped in 1260 by an army of Mamluks, Islamic slave soldiers from Egypt, with at least notional support from the Christian stronghold of Acre. About the same time, civil war broke out in the Mongol empire, yet again over the issue of succession.

After much intense internal conflict, Kublai Khan, a grandson of Genghis, became supreme leader of the Mongols and focused his attention on defeating the Song Chinese. This he achieved in 1279 and, as emperor of the Yuan dynasty ruling all of China, began extensive programs of construction work, especially public schools, ports and roads whilst also encouraging arts, science and trade with Europe. He died in 1294 after which the Mongol empire permanently fractured into independent khanates.

In **China**, the Song dynasty, as previously addressed, capitulated in 1279. The country had, despite being split into northern and southern rule, achieved much under the Song. Rice cultivation expanded dramatically, as did shipbuilding, international trade, paper production – and hence books and documents – and high-quality ceramics. The compass was invented, as was gunpowder, moveable-type printing and paper money. There was a standing conscript army and the first permanent navy was established in 1132, however the public administration was controlled by neither military nor religious elements but was run by a specifically educated elite.

The advent of Kublai Khan's rule – the Yuan dynasty - did not sweep away the institutions and cultural practices of the ethnic Chinese: the reality was the Mongols lacked the numbers and sophistication to do so. Rather, the country was left to run much as it already had, excepting that any positions of authority went to non-Chinese. Whilst

Confucian practices and other religious observances were not restricted, almost everything else was. No weapons were allowed to Chinese, even eating knives; public gatherings were banned and many were forced into hard labour to enable Kublai's extensive building program of roads, canals and public edifices. Intensive agriculture was not something the pastoralist Mongols were well versed in and, whilst rice and cotton production continued successfully, large areas of good agricultural land was converted to pasture. The inevitable consequences were widespread erosion and starvation.

Even before Kublai Khan died in 1294 there was much discontent amongst the populace and central authority was waning. After his death, incompetent rulers accelerated the process and rebel groups were increasingly being formed, especially in the south. The leader of one such rebel group, Zhu Yuanzhang, gained armed superiority over his rivals and, in 1368 proclaimed himself emperor of a new Ming dynasty. Taking his army north, he captured Khanbaliq (Beijing) without a fight and, though it took another thirteen years, he eventually ruled a unified China under Han Chinese rule.

By the end of the Medieval Age, the Ming dynasty was firmly entrenched in the country and largely at peace, although occasionally troublesome at the borders. Of particular concern were ongoing Mongol incursions in the north and that caused a renewed focus on repairing and improving the border wall – the "Great Wall of China". Begun in the Iron Age, this massive feat of engineering was originally constructed of rammed earth with just the occasional use of stone in difficult hilly terrain. During the

Ming dynasty mortared brick and stone were used and this saw two developments: one being the business of mass-production which had to match the demand for an enormous quantity of clay bricks. A second feature, designed to ensure longevity, was the use of "sticky rice" to stabilize and strengthen the mortar. Stretching some 21,000 kilometres the barrier, some nine metres wide and over seven metres tall in places and of which some 6,000 kilometres were completed in the Ming era, remains a marvel to us modern partly-wise persons.

At about the same time as the Chinese Ming dynasty was assuming power over their Mongol overlords, another offshoot of the Mongol horde was looming to spread devastation across western Asia. These were the **Tatars**, and in particular their leader Amir **Temur** (Tamerlane). Born near Samarkand (Uzbekistan), he was in his mid-to-late-thirties when appointed imperial ruler of the Chaghatay Khanate and launched an offensive against the Khorezm to the north. The capital city of Kat was taken; all the males butchered and their wives and children made slaves, while the city was plundered and burned. This was to be the hallmark of Temur's approach over the next three decades: keeping his troops busy but well supplied with booty and meeting any opposition with ruthless cruelty. He next moved south to Khorasan (Iran), sacking the cities of Herat and Kandahar, amongst others, leaving tell-tale pyramids of skulls in his wake. In the city of Isfizar (Iran) he exceeded his previous deeds of cruelty by cementing 2,000 prisoners into a wall whilst still alive. Similar feats of inhumanity followed his pillaging through Persia, Georgia and the Caucasus before turning his attention to India in 1398. Leaving 100,000 skulls on departing the ruined city of Multan (Pakistan) he proceeded to destroy Delhi to such an extent that it would take a century to recover. Damascus in the Levant and Ankara in Turkey suffered similarly before Temur turned his attention toward China in 1405. He died on the way. Amir Temur remains a national hero in his homeland of Uzbekistan.

Any overview of mankind's progress in **India** during the Medieval Age risks descending into a tedious list of dynasties, rivalries and minor conquests – of which there were many of each. Of great significance, though were the Battles of Tarain, north of Delhi, fought in 1191 and 1192. The wealth of India had become well known amongst the Islamic people beyond the mountains of the Hindu Kush and was an accordingly attractive target for acquisition. An Islamic army under a ruling general named Muhammad Ghori (properly Mu'izz ad-Din Muhammad), after some reversals, managed to encircle and capture Lahore (Punjab) in 1186 and realized that Punjab (modern Pakistan) was the best land access to India itself. His army descended on Delhi in 1191 and offered the ruler Rajput Chauhan peace if he accepted subordination and conversion to Islam. This being declined, battle ensued and Ghori was badly defeated but escaped. Retreating and reinforcing his army, he attacked again the following year and, aided by a classic Mongol tactic of feigned withdrawal, managed to defeat Chauhan decisively. Having established Moslem rule over northern, and later north-eastern India, Ghori himself turned for home in 1206 but was assassinated enroute. He left behind what became a series of Islamic dynasties known collectively as the Delhi Sultanate that ruled most of India until the end of the Age.

India was a rich country, although it must be said that the difference between the wealth of the nobility and that of the ordinary worker was enormous. Primarily agricultural in the early years of the Age, overall production, which included cereals and pulses (peas, beans etc), oilseeds and cotton, increased markedly and permitted growth in urban settlement and manufacturing. That led to a revival in trade and during this Age India became a major trading nation. Exports included textiles and brass, copper and iron goods plus more exotic wares such as silk, jewels and pearls. Imports often included significant numbers of Ethiopian slaves, who became known as Hapshis. That latter does indicate the extent of seagoing trade that plied through the Persian Gulf then overland through Mesopotamia and beyond or to Red Sea ports feeding western Europe. China was also a trading partner and in 1405 an imperial Chinese fleet of over three hundred ships travelled a well-charted trade route to India.

One might reasonably wonder at the apparent religious coexistence that generally prevailed between the Islamic invaders and local Hindus. Except when concentrated for military action, though, the Muslims were very much in the minority among the general population and thus needed caution. Equally, and somewhat ironically, "Hindu" was simply the Persian word for "inhabitant of India", so there was no formally acknowledged religion to convert. Indeed, Hinduism, as it has since become known, is more a philosophy and way of life without a rigid structure and relying much on "Karma" [an individual's actions determine their fate] as a guiding force. There were almost certainly forced conversions, adherents killed and temples destroyed, but the more pragmatic Muslim rulers sought to dominate rather than convert.

In the **Americas** the inhabitants lived in isolation from the rest of the world throughout the Medieval Age and one could assert that there was no recognizable medieval civilization. In the far north, though, were the Thule people, ancestors of the Inuit, who expanded east from Alaska into northern Canada and Greenland, living underground in winter and in skin tents in the warmer months. They were practical hunters with few artistic traits and subsisted on whales, caribou, seal and fish.

In the mid-north (now USA) there were doubtless small groups of hunter-gatherer families in the eastern states but evidence is scarce and the known populations of the era were mainly in the west and along the Mississippi River. The oldest is probably that of Cahokia in Illinois with a peak population of some 40,000 living in thatched stone-walled houses and with a large communal or ceremonial mounded platform. They had a corn-based economy but seem to have used copper although evidence is slim and the culture simply vanished toward the end of the period. In the south-west there were three known societies, the Ancestral Puebloans, the Mogollon people and the Hohokam people. The Ancestral Puebloans, known to the later Navajo as "Anasazi", or *ancient enemies,* were a village community with terraced multi-storey buildings with communal space on defensive ledges or mesas. They became known for their decorated pottery. Other tribal groups, mainly hunter-gatherers, that would have traded or come into conflict with the Puebloans included the Utes (Utah/Colorado), Shoshones (Wyoming, Idaho, Nevada, Utah) and the Paiute (California, Nevada/Oregon). In 1130 there began widespread drought across North America lasting some three hundred years. Two particular cultural groups that also existed in the south-west at the beginning of this Age but which had dispersed by its end - the Mogollon and Hohokam people - are likely to have been seriously impacted and that may have caused their demise.

In <u>the Central American</u> region there were two and potentially three great civilizations, all in the region of modern Mexico. The first of these, the Maya, was previously addressed in the Migration Age and continued to occupy the ancient city of Chichen Itza until around 1220. What seems likely is that internal power shifts or civil war then caused the majority of the population to shift some hundred kilometres west to the city of Mayapan. What occurred over the following few hundred years is speculative but by the end of the Medieval Age the Mayan people had dispersed from their existing major cities and occupied scattered, smaller ones. The second civilization in the region was that of the Toltecs who occupied Tula (or Tollau) in the Valley of Mexico. The city itself was certainly substantial, indicating a population of up to 50,000 and with large stone statues and pyramids, very similar to Maya constructions. The city was abandoned and destroyed in 1168. The Aztecs, the third civilization under consideration, claimed descent from the Toltecs although some Wiser Persons have cast doubt on the reality of Toltec existence as a separate grouping. Regardless, the Aztecs certainly existed, and prospered in their impressively luxurious capital city of Tenochtitlan. With an urban population of around 200,000 and ruled by a single emperor with a hierarchy of nobles, the Aztecs were a relatively sophisticated and warlike people, well versed in the use of javelins and spears. They apparently preferred to capture rather than kill their enemies, who were then either enslaved or sacrificed and the army ventured thousands of kilometres from the capital to ensure their dominance and obtain slaves. The renowned Montezuma (Moctezuma II) was the last of their deified emperors reigning in the Medieval Age and before the advent of Spanish conquerors.

In the <u>south of the Americas</u> a significant number of tribal groups, largely in the Patagonian region, were mixed hunter-gatherers and/or basic farmers with others such as the now-extinct Yamanas people of the extreme south collecting seafoods and harpoon fishing from bark canoes. Further north there were scattered settlements growing corn and sweet potatoes, with larger ones using metal tools and crafting in silver and copper. The largest known of such settlements, enjoying a population of around 5,000, was that of the Quilmes (Kilmes) people of Calchaqui Valley (NW Argentina). Originating around the year 700, the Quilmes people survived as an independent society until about 1475 when they were conquered and assimilated into the Incan Empire.

The Incas populated most of the western seaboard of South America in this period, with a realm then known as *Tawantinsuyu* controlled from the city-state of Cusco (renamed Peru by the Spanish). Comprising mainly disparate tribal pastoralists the Incas developed a remarkably advanced empire despite being linguistically diverse and having no written language. They built in stone (notably the citadel of Machu Picchu, 80km NW of Cusco), worshipped a Sun God and had a societal organization based primarily around barter, individual work obligations and a dogma forbidding stealing, lying and laziness. The empire began expanding from Cusco around 1438 and though ravaged by various outbreaks of disease (Smallpox, Influenza, Measles, Diphtheria etc) thrived until conquered by the Spanish in 1572.

There are more limited definitions, but **Central Asia** may be considered for our partly-wise purposes as being the bulk of that landmass which is distant from oceans on Earth's largest continent. Its geography varies from mountains to deserts but is mainly treeless grassy steppes suffering extremes of temperature and low rainfall. The medieval population was scattered and tribal, a wide mix of Huns, Turks, Scythians, Persians and Mongols amongst others, with a common thread being their nomadic livestock-herding way of life. They did have one significant advantage – the horse. These steppe horses were as tough as their owners were forced to be in that demanding Asian environment. When combined with stirrups, composite recurve bow and sword or lasso the rider and horse constituted a formidable fighting machine. Whether they were inherently warlike people is debatable, but when faced with a foe they demonstrated courage, aggression and great tactical skill.

Another Asian pairing of man and animal was the Arab and his camel (camel drivers were rarely female). Long domesticated, the camel has similar environmental hardiness to the steppe horse but can last longer without water and carry heavier loads. It was thus well suited to long-distance carriage of goods and became the common carrier over the 11,000 kilometres or so of the **Silk Road**, principally between places such as Antioch in the Levant and Khanbaliq (Beijing) or Karakorum in Mongolia. Trade between Europe and China flourished throughout the Medieval Age, interrupted only partly when the Ottoman (Turkish) Empire cut off trade with western Europe in 1453 whilst continuing the trade eastwards. Logically, trade goods on the varying routes involved were lightweight and high value. Typically, they would include silk, tea, cotton textiles, gemstones, lacquerware and spices. Horses and slaves, especially girls, were also traded, and as silver coinage was not then common, silk itself became a form of currency. The trade route carried other less visible traffic, namely plague, cultural knowledge and religion.

The need also arose along the Silk Road for overnight shelter and protection of the valuable camel trains that crisscrossed the steppes and these 'caravansaries' as they became known provided a basis for walled settlements in otherwise barren landscapes. Some became towns and a tribal people known as the Sogdians, focusing almost exclusively on trade from their original base in Samarkand (Uzbekistan), had developed what amounted to minor city-states in strategic oases along the route. There were thus sedentary populations in parts of Central Asia as well as the more well-known nomadic tribes.

Despite conflicts, massacres and plagues, Earth's population had risen to around 500 million by the end of the Medieval Age.

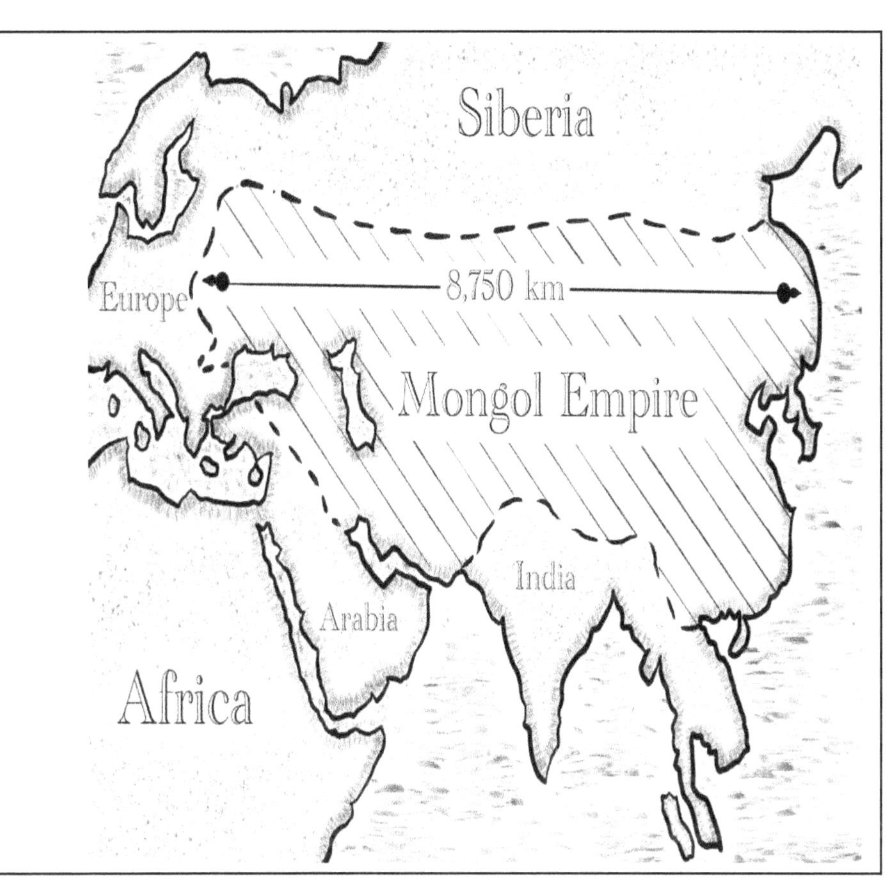

Fig 6: Mongol Empire in the time of Kublai Khan

MEDIEVAL AGE – MILESTONES 1000 - 1500

11TH CENTURY

1004 – Chinese Song emperor concludes treaty with Mongol raiders: includes annual payments of silk and over 280 kilograms of silver.

1013 – Danes conquer England. Sweyn Forkbeard crowned but reigns only five weeks. King Ethelred returns from refuge in Normandy and reigns briefly until Canute (Knut) crowned, beginning nearly three decades of Danish rule.

1040 – Macbeth murders King Duncan of Scotland and succeeds him for fourteen years.

First movable type (using porcelain) introduced in Chinese Song   Dynasty

1043 – Edward (the Confessor) crowned king of England.

1054 – East and West Christian churches break apart.

1065 – Westminster Abbey (London) consecrated.

1066 – Halley's Comet appears.

William (the Conqueror) of Normandy invades England, crowned king.

1075 – Seljuk Turks subdue Syria and Palestine.

1084 – Synod (church assembly) of Rome deposes Pope Gregory, recognizes anti-Pope Clement II. Normans sack Rome.

1086 – Shen Kua of China invents a magnetic compass suitable for navigation.

Domesday Book (Inventory of England) compiled.

1095 – Byzantine emperor Alexius requests aid to combat Seljuk Turks.

Pope Urban declares a crusade.

1096 – First Crusade to the Holy Land of about 30,000 men.

1099 – Crusaders capture Jerusalem: kill 40,000 Jews and Muslims; destroy mosques and synagogues.

12th CENTURY

1120 – Henry I of England makes peace with Louis VI of France.

Order of Knights Templar formally established in Jerusalem.

1130 - Widespread drought in North America**.**

1132 – China established its first permanent navy.

1139 – Civil war in England: King Stephen v Empress Matilda; lasts 14 years.

Pope Innocent II at 2nd Lateran Council outlaws jousts, tournaments and "that murderous art of crossbowmen and archers" against Christians. These edicts are widely ignored.

1147 - Second Crusade begins with some 500,000 crusaders.

1150 - Temple complex of Angkor Wat, perhaps the largest in the world, completed in Cambodia about this time.

1151 – First known fire and plague insurance policy issued in Iceland.

1152 – Eleanor of Aquitaine's marriage to Louis VII annulled; she marries Henry Duke of Normandy who becomes King of England 1154.

1156 – Pope Adrian IV (the only English Pope) grants approval for Henry II of England to invade and rule Ireland "for setting bounds to the progress of wickedness".

1168 – Toltec city of Tula (Valley of Mexico) is abandoned.

1180 – Civil war breaks out in Japan with Minamoto v Taira Samurai clans vying for power. Minamoto clan victorious by

1185 which introduces Shogunates (military governments) at expense of Emperor's power.

1187 – Saladin defeats crusader forces at Battle of Hattin, takes Jerusalem.

1189 – Hundreds of Jews are massacred in England when eviction from King Richard's coronation feast fuels rumours that the king wants them gone. Overturning debt owed to Jewish moneylenders had much to do with it.

1191 – Third Crusade begins.

1192 – Islamic force defeats Indian force at Battle of Tarain near Delhi, establishing Muslim rule over northern India.

1194 – Major flooding in China dramatically alters the course of the Yellow River which remains on changed route for nearly 700 years.

1200 – City of Cuzco (Peru) founded by Incas. Maya culture dies out.

13TH CENTURY

1202 – 4th Crusade begins. Venice provides ships in return for sacking Zara (now Zada, Croatia) plus half the booty obtained in the venture. (Evidently not all crusade supporters had religious motives).

1204 – Crusaders sack Constantinople. Crusade to Holy Land fails.

1206 – Temujin (aged 44) proclaimed Genghis Khan at Karakorum.

1211 – Genghis Khan invades China: captures Beijing 1214.

1215 – Magna Carta (a charter of rights) sealed at Runnymede (England) between an unpopular King John and rebel barons establishing a foundation for a rule of law in England.

1222 – Mongol forces reach Russia, defeat Russian army 1223 then retreat.

1227 – Genghis Khan dies.

Porcelain manufacturing begins in Japan, initially using Chinese techniques.

1229 – A Council of Toulouse (S. France), seeking to stop heresies spreading through unauthorized bibles, barred lay persons from possessing old and new Testaments.

1231 – Pope Gregory IX, attempting to control treatment of heresy, which was then a state crime, introduces a formal Inquisition or trial by clergy.

Japanese Shogun forbids sale of children into slavery.

1237 – Mongols use gunpowder; devastate Poland; capture Moscow. They then threaten Western Europe, defeating Teutonic Knights in Silesia (Poland) in 1241 but retreat when Ogedai Khan dies.

1247 – Hungarians found city of Buda to replace city of Pest destroyed by Mongols.

1249 – Seventh Crusade invades Egypt: massacred within a few months.

1252 – European Inquisition authorized by Pope to use torture.

1260 – Chinese Yuan dynasty founded by Kublai Khan.

1271 – Italian Marco Polo joins father and uncle on travels for India and   China.

1274 – Kublai Khan invades Japan with large fleet but fails due to typhoon; same occurs again in 1281, both times with major losses.

1284 – Vietnamese repulse an invading Chinese army – the second of three failed attempts ordered by Kublai Khan.

1290 – King Edward I issues edict expelling all Jews from England (effectively about 3,000), largely to erase debt. This remains in effect for 366 years.

1300 – The "Little Ice Age" begins, a 500-year period, varying regionally, marked by generally lower (2C) temperatures. In Europe cooler summers reduced crop yields.

14th CENTURY

1307 – The Knights Templar are suppressed in France and England. Within five years they are formally abolished and their Grand Master burned at the stake for heresy.

1314 – Scots king Robert Bruce defeats Edward II at Battle of Bannockburn, ultimately leading to recognition of Scottish independence in 1328.

1315 – Widespread famine in Europe: persists for about three years.

1320 – Maori people from Polynesia begin settling New Zealand.

1321 – Civil war breaks out in England between Edward II and the Marcher (Welsh border) barons. Edward is victorious but discontent continues under his harsh rule until his wife Queen Isabella and her lover invade from France in 1326 and assume power.

1325 – Aztec capital city of Tenochtitlan (Mexico City) founded about this time

1333 – Black Death evident in China.

1337 – Hundred Years War begins between England and France, although preceded by hostilities at sea the previous year. Dispute essentially over rival claims to French throne. Hostilities wax and wane over next 116 years.

1344 – Yellow River in China floods, changes direction and causes massive devastation.

1346 – Battle of Crecy (France).

1348 – Plague (Black Death) widespread through Europe.

1356 – Battle of Poitiers (France).

1358 – Peasants' revolt ("Jacquerie") arises in France. Oppressive rule and taxes, discontent over the comparative wealth of nobles and political instability all played their part. Similar elements could be seen in the peasants' revolt in England which occurred 23 years later (1381). Both were ruthlessly put down.

1362 – English "Pleading Act" requires that pleas, debates and judgements in courts be in English rather than French and be recorded in Latin.

1368 – Chinese rebel declares himself emperor of new Ming dynasty; drives Mongols from Beijing.

1378 – The Papal Schism begins with two popes (in Avignon and Rome), and later a third (in Pisa), contesting the position. Not resolved until 1417 when an entirely different pope – Martin V - was elected, reigning in Rome.

1380 – Timur (Tamerlane) begins his violent formation of a Timurid Empire, conquering Afghanistan, Central Asia, Persia, the Caucasus and Georgia. His expansionist devastation, including of northern India, continues to the end of the Medieval Age.

1391 – Geoffrey Chaucer writes "Canterbury Tales".

1392 – Korea (then Choson) becomes a kingdom with capital at Hanyang (Seoul).

1399 – Henry Bolingbroke, denied his accession as Duke of Lancaster, captures and imprisons King Richard II and assumes the throne of England as Henry IV.

15TH CENTURY

1405 - Chinese Zheng He begins exploratory voyages (initially 63 ships) encompassing Sumatra, Ceylon (Sri Lanka), East Africa, Hormuz (Iran) and Aden.

1406 – Translation into Latin of Claudius Ptolemy's work "Geography" revives European thinking that the Earth is spherical.

1429 – Joan of Arc helps liberate Orleans (France). She is captured a year later by English allies, tried and then burned at the stake aged 19. Subsequently cleared of wrongdoing she was ultimately canonized in 1920.

1433 – China enters period of national isolation after Zheng He returns from his final voyage of exploration.

1434 – Portuguese begin trading slaves from West Africa.

1438 – Incas begin expansion of empire along western seaboard of S. America from city-state of Cusco (Cuzco) (SE Peru).

1450 – Trading city of Great Zimbabwe (SE Africa) abandoned; cause unknown.

1453 – Constantinople falls to Ottoman forces.
100-Years War ends with English losing all lands in France except Calais.

1455 – War of the Roses erupts in England.

1456 – Ottoman Turks occupy Athens and rule what later became Greece.

1475 – First printed cookbook appears in Italy entitled "Concerning honest pleasure and well-being".

1477 – Cricket is banned in England for interfering in archery practice.

1487 – Aztecs consecrate Main Temple at Tenochtitlan with some 4,000 humans sacrificed. These sacrifices are repeated at a rate of about 20,000 annually.

1488 – Portuguese navigator Bartholomeu Dias rounds the southern tip of Africa for the first time by a European.

1489 – Symbols for plus (+) and minus (-) first appear in print.

1492 – Italian Christopher Columbus sets sail from Spain westwards in search of trade route to East Indies (SE Asia). Lands in the Bahamas, apparently believing it in the Orient, and establishes Spanish colony at Hispaniola (Haiti/Dominican Republic).

1493 – Second voyage of Columbus, financed by sale of Jewish assets in Spain. Lands in Cuba and subsequently in Jamaica

1494 - Treaty of Tordesillas between Portugal and Spain divides ownership of all newly discovered lands between them. Treaty ignored by other European powers.

1497 – Italian seaman John Cabot commissioned by Henry VII of England, lands in North America (probably Newfoundland).
Leonardo da Vinci paints "The Last Supper".

1498 – Portuguese Vasco da Gama lands in Calicut (Kozhikode, India), establishing a sea route from Europe to India for the first time.

EXPLORATION AGE: 1500 – 1750

There are Wiser Persons who have referred to this period as the Age of Discovery, which may be accurate from a purely European perspective, but the existing inhabitants of the newly 'discovered' lands would properly consider any such discovery to have been made by their own forebears many centuries previously. Herein it becomes the Exploration Age, as that exploration activity is a particular and notable characteristic of the period. Other marked characteristics included issues surrounding religion and slavery, hence rather than a geographic approach, it may be useful to address this period in a more subjective manner.

Exploration.

The enablers of international exploration were already falling into place in the 15th Century. The magnetic compass was in regular use, knowledge of astronomy combined with use of the astrolabe (predecessor to the sextant) allowed calculation of latitude and there was increasing expertise in the navigation of ships, especially amongst the Portuguese. The final element required, other than a means of calculating longitude, was the ocean-going vessel. It was the Portuguese who also came to the fore in this regard with their design of the Caravel. This relatively light – usually 60-100 tons – fast and agile style of sailing vessel had proven well suited to the Mediterranean and coastal African trade and could manage both ocean passages and inshore surveying. Though they would later be overtaken by the larger galleons of Britain and Spain for warlike purposes and by 1,000-ton Carracks for bulk trade, the Caravel was ideal for exploration. Two of the vessels in Columbus's first voyage across the Atlantic were Caravels.

Despite those enablers, what was previously missing was a driving motivation to explore, above and beyond that of mere curiosity. That was provided by the Ottomans who then not only controlled Egypt and thus the Red Sea route to the East but also, in 1453, had cut, or at least severely diminished, European access to the Silk Road. This stranglehold on access to trade goods to which Europeans had become accustomed was sufficient in itself to demand action to find an alternative. Competition for land and resource acquisition between the European maritime powers provided further impetus. The Portuguese were the first to make serious progress in maritime exploration with Bartolomeu Dias sailing around the southern tip of Africa in 1488 and Vasco da Gama voyaging to India a decade later. This was key to future European access to SE Asia and the spice islands, although the feat pales in comparison to that of the Chinese Admiral Zheng He, whose fleet had explored most of the countries bordering the Indian Ocean as far as Africa almost a century earlier.

Of perhaps greater long-term significance was the identification of a "New World" across the Atlantic. Credit for this is routinely accorded to the Italian Christopher Columbus in 1492, although almost anyone who sailed westward from Europe would have inevitably struck the land mass we know as the Americas in due course. Even then, Columbus' navigational ability was highly suspect if he seriously believed, as was then asserted, that he had landed in the East Indies. Nonetheless, his reports of what we now know as the Caribbean Islands triggered a flurry of exploratory voyages by Europeans such as John Cabot, Vasco da Gama, Ferdinand Magellan and Francis Drake. It would take many more years of exploration, though, for Europe to grasp the enormity of the land mass that comprised the Americas.

By agreement between Spain and Portugal the former could claim ownership of newly found lands west of a demarcation line that ran through what is now Brazil whilst Portugal retained ownership of eastern Brazil and western Africa. What followed was conquest, colonization, and exploitation by both nations. From their series of bases in the Caribbean the Spanish expanded westward into South America and Mexico, conquering the Aztec and Inca empires in the process. By 1540 Spanish expeditions had explored much of south-western North America inland across the Rocky Mountains as far as modern-day Kansas. Florida, to the south-east, was colonized in 1564. Meanwhile Portugal had established its first permanent settlement in the Americas at Sao Vicente (Brazil) and a series of lesser colonies along the Brazilian coast which were ultimately amalgamated with a capital at San Salvador. By 1567 Rio de Janeiro was founded and sugar cane was an established Brazilian export. Coffee seeds would take another 160 years to arrive.

Conscious of Spanish and Portuguese strength to the south, other European powers, notably Britain and France, focused their exploratory and colonization efforts on eastern North America. Their early efforts, including failure to identify any north-west passage across to the

Pacific, involved great hardship and were largely fruitless. The first English settlement at Jamestown (Virginia) in 1607 involved few with any relevant skills and they had to endure drought, disease, starvation and an increasingly hostile native population once they began to expand. By 1700, however, England had established twelve relatively small colonies along the eastern seaboard and one more – Savannah, Georgia – was added in 1733. By 1750 the population of those colonies had increased to around 1.5 million, a growing proportion of whom were slaves or convicts. There was virtually no, or at least very limited, English overland exploration westward. French colonists explored much further inland. From an initial fur trading post on the St Lawrence River (Quebec) in 1600, French colonists ventured as far west as modern Ontario and Manitoba, whilst pushing south through what are now Ohio and Illinois to Louisiana on the Gulf of Mexico, establishing New Orleans in 1718 and Baton Rouge two years later. They were great builders of forts wherever they went, although their relationships with the native Americans they encountered seem to have been relatively peaceful.

Exploration of the south-west Pacific was patchy during this Age. The Straits of Malacca were known as a gateway to the Pacific as early as the 15th century and both Malacca itself (Malaya) and later Jakarta (Indonesia) were early trading ports, especially for spices such as nutmeg and cloves. That trade was enormously profitable and monopolized both Portuguese and Dutch interest, with much mutual conflict and largely to the exclusion of exploration. It was not until 1606 when the Dutch seafarer Willem Janszoon, in search of additional trade outlets, landed on Cape York Peninsula that Europeans became aware of a land to the south of New Guinea, although Janszoon then thought the two lands connected. It was another 21 years before another Dutchman, Abel Tasman, searching for the hypothetical *"Terra Australis"*, sailing around Australia but well offshore and out of sight, identified the islands of Tasmania (then Van Diemen's Land), New Zealand and Fiji. Tasman revisited Australia in 1644, charting the north coast, but that was the last of the exploratory visits to Australasia during this Age.

Slavery.

The practice of "owning" other humans and enforcing their labour in one form or another has been evident in human society ever since records began. It is significant in this Age because trans-Atlantic slavery became so egregious and patently dehumanizing that the groundwork was laid for its ultimate international abolition.

There were two particular factors at play in the Americas that initially triggered the demand for labour: sugar and tobacco. Both are labour intensive crops to produce and harvest and, in the climatic conditions those crops grow best, European settlers were unsuited to the work. Progressive introduction of cotton plantations after 1500 and coffee in the 18th century exacerbated the problem. Subjugation and enslavement of the native population was a solution in the south, but initially doomed to failure, even if considered, in the northern colonies. Decimation of the local people by introduced smallpox further aggravated the labour situation. The solution was importation of slaves from Africa.

The Portuguese were the first to embark on trans-Atlantic slavery, although Spanish interests were the primary customers. Trading captured African tribespeople in West Africa for muskets and manufactured goods, the captives were then shipped in 1503 to the Spanish colony of Hispaniola in the Caribbean to harvest sugar cane. As Spanish settlements in Brazil expanded the demand for labour increased and this was accelerated in 1542 when King Charles I of Spain introduced "New Laws" which prohibited the enslavement of "Indians".

In 1562 the English privateer John Hawkins traded 300 African slaves for produce, including sugar, and returned to England advocating involvement in what was seen as a lucrative opportunity. Thereafter, almost all major European powers were involved in the trading of African slaves across the Atlantic. This trade existed with both the knowledge and acquiescence of European authorities. As early as 1452 Pope Nicholas V sanctioned the reduction of non-Christians to "perpetual servitude" in his Papal Bull *"Dum Diversas"*. Similarly, Charles V, the Holy Roman Emperor and King of Spain granted charters for the transport of slaves and Elizabeth I of England actually financially supported the slaving pursuits of John Hawkins. Many other notables of history such as Francis Drake, Christopher Columbus and George Washington were actively involved in slavery to some degree: the practice was not unusual. This was also so within the North American colonies, with almost 5,000 enslaved Native Americans ("Indians") shipped from South Carolina to other colonies between 1670 and 1715.

What was relatively unusual was the degree of degradation and misery to which enslaved Africans were subjected during their trans-Atlantic voyage, often lasting up to three months. Chained and crammed together by the hundreds in confined holds with little or no room for movement, they were forced to lie in their own excrement and vomit whilst being fed just sufficient to survive. Unsurprisingly some ten percent or more of the many millions so transported died on the journey, mainly from dysentery.

Slavery was not ultimately abolished in any legal sense until 1833 by Britain (*Slavery Abolition Act*); 1835 by Spain; 1865 by the United States (*13th Amendment to the Constitution*) and 1869 by Portugal for its African colonies.

Religion.

At the beginning and for much of this Age of Exploration, Europe was in a maelstrom of wars and internal domestic conflicts. Much of the conflict ostensibly had its basis in religion but the reality was often more about disputed power and control.

In 1500 Europe was Catholic Christian. That did not mean any degree of religious unity prevailed, even setting aside the continued rift with the Eastern Orthodox church following the Schism of the 11th Century. The papacy was weak and only slowly recovering from the Western Schism of the previous century when two simultaneous and competing Popes claimed office. The clamor for reform was widespread, often frustrated by vested interests and clerical corruption, whilst abuse of office was entrenched.

Matters came to a head in 1517 when a German monk named Martin Luther took advantage of the relatively new opportunities provided by the printing press to spread his protests and demand for reforms. Thus was Protestantism born and Luther's particular approach became known as "Lutheran", whilst a similarly influential figure John Calvin birthed a more uncompromising form of Protestantism which became known as "Calvinism". The Protestant movement spread rapidly across northern Europe.

Meanwhile, in England, King Henry VIII was having trouble begetting an heir and equal difficulty in getting the Pope to dissolve what had until then been deemed his perfectly valid marriage. Henry was well versed in ecclesiastical matters, having been awarded the title Defender of the Faith *("Fide Defense")* for a treatise repudiating Lutheranism (a title still rather cynically claimed by British monarchs of today based upon a parliamentary award). His solution in 1534 was to espouse Protestantism and have parliament pass an Act of Supremacy making him and his successors head of the Church of England. There were financial benefits. What followed was an Act of Dissolution whereby England's convents, priories and monasteries were closed, many destroyed, and their assets and incomes claimed by the crown.

After Henry died in 1547 a brief period of Catholicism arose again in England when Mary assumed the throne and peace with Spain was achieved through her subsequent marriage to Philip II of Spain. Protestantism officially returned when she died and Elizabeth, Anne Boleyn's daughter, was crowned and continued until

Charles I's reign from 1625. A Catholic uprising in Ireland in 1641 and a muted royal response inflamed long festering feuding with parliament and civil war ensued. Charles was defeated by Puritan Oliver Cromwell and executed, introducing an 11-year period of republicanism. Subsequent to the restoration of the monarchy in 1660, another brief period found a Catholic monarch on the throne, this being James II (James VII of Scotland). His rule was equally fraught in terms of his relationship with parliament and attempts to assert his authority, combined with the birth of a son that raised the prospect of a Catholic dynasty, led to his downfall. What followed was an unusual mix between a coup and an invasion when his son-in-law, William of Orange (married to James' eldest daughter Mary), was invited to assume the "vacated" throne as William III. William then spent much of his joint reign with Mary on the mainland in war with France. James' younger daughter Anne, similarly brought up Protestant, assumed the throne on William's death and upon an Act of 1707 (*Acts of Union* between England and Scotland) became the first queen of Great Britain and Ireland.

In mainland Europe over a third of the population either became Protestant or, more accurately, and as in the rest of the world over the ages, what others decreed their religion would be. Conflicts arose between Catholic and Protestant interests and those conflicts were not always based upon religious conviction. Key individuals in much of what occurred were the Habsburgs, an originally German Catholic dynasty. By a tangled web of marriages and agreements Charles of the Habsburgs became Lord of the Netherlands in 1506; inherited the crown of Spain and ruler of Austria in 1516; and three years later Holy Roman Emperor. This large Habsburg empire was challenging to manage and beset on all sides: growing Protestant independence movements to the north in the Netherlands and Germany; ongoing threat from the Ottomans in the east; and hostile neighbours to the west in France and Britain. The empire was almost constantly in a state of hostilities with one or other European power throughout the Age. Perhaps unsurprisingly, Charles abdicated in 1556 due to ill health and passed his responsibilities to Ferdinand for Austria, Bohemia (Czech Republic) and Hungary and to his son Philip II for Spain. That latter country, staunchly Catholic and already a powerful nation with many valuable overseas territories, found itself in almost continuous conflict with the Dutch and English. This was despite a brief marriage alliance with Catholic Mary I of England (1554-1558).

France was having its own problems in this period. Around ten percent of the population had espoused Protestantism, with two principal factions comprising a moderate Lutheran congregation in the east and a more extreme Calvinist grouping in the south-west which included many of the nobility and became known as Huguenots. The country was also at war over its possessions in Italy, initially allied with, but then against, Venice but mainly pitted against the Papacy, Holy Roman Empire, Spain and Swiss mercenaries. England also declared against France, opportunistically invading to recover its lost lands in Aquitaine (SW France) although that endeavour failed badly.

Complicating matters in France was an extant "Pragmatic Sanction", a form of royal edict, which planned to restrict, and partially remove, the authority of the Pope over internal French religious matters. Compromise was achieved after a significant French military victory over papal and allied forces with a "Concordat" between King Francis I and Pope Leo X in 1516. This, inter alia, retained papal authority in what would remain a Catholic France but provided for the monarch to appoint senior clergy. Tensions between Catholics and Huguenots and conflict between Huguenots and the monarchy not only continued but worsened, peaking in 1572 with a massacre of many thousands of Huguenots. It was not until 1598 that some measure of peace was attained with an edict (Edict of Nantes) that provided civil rights to members of the "Reformed" religion. This didn't last. The edict was revoked in 1685 so that Protestantism in France remained forbidden for another century. This aligned France with most other European (and many other) powers whereby the only religion permitted in the country was that authorized by the State.

China

Not especially troubled by issues of exploration, slavery or religion was the burgeoning nation of China. Early in the Age the Ming Dynasty was progressing slowly toward financial collapse. Matters had begun well: agricultural production was improving; arts and literature were flourishing as was trade, notably exports of porcelain, silk and spices through the Spanish galleon traders based in Manila (Philippines). Rapid population growth, inept administration and a lavishly expensive imperial family increased costs, whilst poor harvests, occasional famine and epidemics together with assiduous tax avoidance reduced income. To make matters worse campaigns against Japan and Korea had proven costly and inhibited trade, whilst conflict then arose with Spain. The Spanish had colonized the Philippines (named after Philip II of Spain) around 1565 and became dependent upon Chinese immigrants to manage and support the galleon trade through Manila. Local resentment, sanctions and excessive taxation of the resident Chinese there led to a major Chinese uprising in 1603 which resulted in some 30,000 resident Chinese being killed and a hiatus in trade with Spain. That loss of income, mainly in the form of silver from the Americas, was very damaging to an already fragile Chinese economy.

In the late 1630s the weakened Ming Dynasty came under threat from a tribal (Jurchen) people from Manchuria to the north-east which re-named themselves "Manchu". They took Beijing in 1644 and despite sporadic resistance progressed south with ruthless efficiency and by 1669 China was under Manchu rule. Their rule, once established, proved to be conservative, efficient and effective, although Han Chinese were discriminated against and exposure to the outside world still severely controlled. Nonetheless, by the end of the Age China had grown its population to around 225 million – over a quarter of the entire world's – was probably the world's wealthiest nation and was exacting tribute from a wide range of other nations.

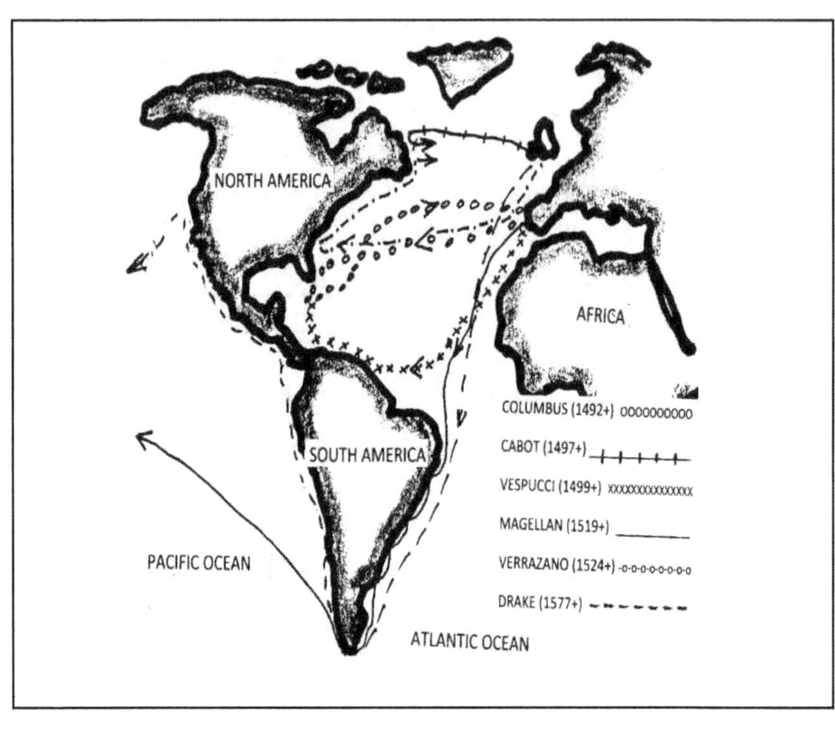

Fig 7: - Atlantic Voyages Late 15th, Early 16th Century

EXPLORATION AGE – MILESTONES
1500-1750

16TH CENTURY

1503 – African slaves are imported into Spanish colony of Hispaniola (W Indies) to harvest sugar cane: first arrival of African slaves in the Americas.
Leonardo da Vinci begins painting *"Mona Lisa"*.
1504 – Michelangelo's statue *"David"* is first displayed.
1509 – Portuguese colonise Porto Seguro, first European settlement in Brazil.
1516 – Sugar mill established in Hispaniola: becomes major export to Spain.
Thomas Moore publishes *"Utopia"*.
1517 – Reformation movement seeking to correct errors and abuses in the western Catholic church begins.
1522 – Portuguese Ferdinand Magellan's ship completes first circumnavigation of the globe. 93 percent of those who originally sailed, (including Magellan) died in the process.
1534 – English king Henry VIII signs Act of Supremacy establishing the monarch as also head of the church.
1543 – Nicolaus Copernicus publishes *"On the Revolutions of Heavenly Bodies"* that first asserts that the earth rotates around own axis and the sun not vice versa. Widely disparaged by theologians such as Martin Luther.
1556 – Deadliest known earthquake strikes Shaanxi China causing massive and widespread damage and over 800,000 deaths.

1562 – John Hawkins, English privateer, trades 300 slaves at Hispaniola for sugar, pearls and ginger, thus involving England in the slave trade.

1564 – Queen Elizabeth I takes shares in Hawkins' slave venture and lends him a ship. She had previously declared that *"if any African were carried away without his free consent it would be detestable and call down the vengeance of Heaven"*.

1565 – Portuguese found colonies of Rio de Janeiro in Brazil and Cebu in the Philippines.

John Hawkins introduces tobacco from Florida (N America) into England.

1569 – Flemish cartographer Gerardus Mercator produces first world map using his "Mercator" projection of rhumb lines which allow for straight-line navigation.

1571 – Battle of Lepanto: last significant naval battle involving oared galleys with over 200 Papal vessels (mainly Spanish and Venetian) destroying similar Ottoman fleet. Over 40,000 lives were lost and some 10,000 Turkish prisoners taken.

1572 – Spanish forces defeat Incas in western S. America.

1580 – Spain invades Portugal, defeats Portuguese forces. Countries remain autonomous but with single (Spanish) monarch for sixty years.

1588 – Spanish armada of 134 ships sails for invasion of England, delayed after Walter Raleigh burns part of the fleet in Cadiz harbour. The fleet is defeated at sea by English fleet.

1589 – English clergyman William Lee invents first knitting machine for production of stockings.

1590 – Shakespeare presents the play *"Henry VI"* (Part 2 then Part 3 and later part 1).

1599 – English East India Company formed to make annual trade voyages.

17th CENTURY

1601 – First East India Company fleet sails, reaches Sumatra (Indonesia), captures a Portuguese trader and returns with a profitable cargo of spices, mainly pepper, in 1603.

1604 – French colonist and explorer Samuel de Champlain explores and charts Atlantic coast of North America; later founds Quebec and 'New France'.

1606 – First European landing in Australia. Dutch ship *Duyfken* attempts settlement at Cape Keerweer (Gulf of Carpentaria) but is repulsed by local natives.

1607 – First permanent English settlement in N America at Jamestown (nr Williamsburg Virginia). Struggled to survive until tobacco exported in 1612.

1613 – Japanese voyage of exploration: visits Acapulco, New Spain (Mexico).

1616 – Notre Dame cathedral built.

1617 – Smallpox decimates Indian population of New England.

1620 – Cargo ship *Mayflower* arrives Cape Cod (Massachusetts) with 102 pilgrims, farmers and servants escaping religious intolerance in Europe. Survivors of the first year (about half) held America's first Thanksgiving dinner in 1621.

1630 – Boston (Massachusetts) is founded by about 1,000 reformist Puritans.

1632 – Construction of Taj Mahal in Agra, India, commissioned by Mughal emperor. Takes some 21 years to complete.

1633 – Galileo tried for heresy by Catholic Inquisitor for advocating Copernicus' theory of Earth revolving around the Sun. Threatened with torture, he recants.

1638 – Japan adopts policy of isolation; prohibits construction of oceangoing vessels.

English clergyman John Howard leaves library at New Town – renamed Cambridge – to seminary: college is named Harvard.

1642 – Dutchman Abel Tasman circumnavigates Australia, sights Tasmania (which he names Van Diemen's Land), New Zealand and Fiji.

1643 - Barometer invented (Italy).

1644 – Chinese Manchu forces take Beijing, end Ming dynasty, begin Qing dynasty.

1645 – Puritan Oliver Cromwell defeats royalist forces in England; later abolishes the monarchy and becomes (1653) Lord Protector of England, Scotland and Ireland.

1652 – Dutch found Cape Town, South Africa.

1660 - Restoration of the monarchy in Britain: Charles II resumes throne.

1664 – Niew Amsterdam is re-named New York after capitulation of Dutch settlers to a British naval force.

1666 – Isaac Newton invents calculus and establishes laws of gravity.

Great Fire of London – 80% of city destroyed.

Italian Antonio Stradivari begins making violins (Stradivarius).

1676 - Greenwich Observatory established to fix standard time.

1678 - John Bunyan writes *"The Pilgrim's Progress"*.

1682 - English Quaker William Penn establishes Pennsylvania (N America).

1683 - Chinese Qing dynasty conquers Taiwan.

1684 – English East India Company establish trading station at Canton (Guangzhou, S China).

1688 – Lloyds of London marine insurance brokerage founded.

1692 – Salem witch trials conducted in Massachusetts – nineteen hanged over two years, mostly on evidence of a 12yo girl.

1699 – English explorer and privateer William Dampier explores NW coast of Australia, having briefly visited there eleven years previously.

18th CENTURY

1701 – Ashanti tribal leader establishes powerful W African empire (modern Ghana) based on gold and slaves.

1702 – Concept of national territory extending 3 miles offshore formulated (Netherlands).

1704 – N America's first regular newspaper (The Boston News-Letter) published.

English forces take Gibraltar from Spain.

1707 – Act of Union combines England (including Wales) with Scotland to form The Kingdom of Great Britain.

1709 – Inexplicably cold winter in Europe (-12 to -15C) freezes rivers, kills crops, generates widespread famine.

1714 – Smallpox inoculation methodology published.

1720 – "South Sea Bubble" bursts. The South Sea Company, in return for a large loan to government and underwriting the national debt, had been given a monopoly on trade with S America and "the South Seas". Rampant speculation, much alleged corruption and little trade eventuated and the share price collapsed with great economic loss.

1722 – Dutch explorer lands on Rapa Nui, names it Easter Island.

1726 – Spanish colonists found city of Montevideo.
Jonathon Swift writes *Gulliver's Travels*.

1730 – Englishman John Harrison presents his design of a marine chronometer accurate enough to enable longitude to be determined.

1733 – British colony of Savannah, Georgia, founded (last of the thirteen British N American colonies).

1735 – Georgia bans imports of rum and slaves.

1736 – First recorded (successful) appendectomy.

1740 – Irish famine: potato crops fail in extreme cold; mass starvation kills up to 20% of the population.

1741 – British fleet and N American colonial infantry attack Spanish Cartagena (Colombia). Minor success but withdraw when disease kills much of the force.

1742 – Swede Anders Celsius devises the Celsius temperature scale.
Handel composes the *"Messiah"*.

1744 – Lord Anson returns to England after a round-the-world voyage having lost most of his crew to scurvy.
Gyroscope stabiliser invented.

1747 – Scottish naval surgeon pioneers treatment for scurvy.

INDEPENDENCE AGE: 1750 - 1850

This period is most often referred to by Wiser Persons as "The Industrial Age" or the "Industrial Revolution". Whilst it is certainly accurate to mark the beginnings of industrialization as occurring in this period, a more dominating influence of the period was a clamor for both national and domestic independence. In terms of the ongoing progress of humanity, the apparent fervor for independence was almost universal whereas industrialization was largely, and certainly initially, limited to Britain and North America. Hence the title.

Europe

The Age opened with tensions brewing throughout Europe over territorial control and relative power perceived to be threatening individual countries' national interests. A significant shift in alliances then saw Britain allying with Hanover (N Germany) and Prussia (SE Baltic) whilst, countering that, France allied herself with Austria and Russia. Outright war broke out in 1756 (the "Seven Years' War"), although hostilities had actually begun in North America two years previously when a young British colonial officer named George Washington attacked a French patrol in Pennsylvania. The ensuing war was global in nature, horrific in terms of property damage and loss of life and destructive of the economies of both Britain and France. By the time peace treaties were negotiated in 1763 (*Treaty of Paris*), Britain was firmly established as the pre-eminent global maritime power and both Britain and France were severely short of funds. Spain, which had belatedly chosen to support French interests and opportunistically but unsuccessfully invaded Britain's ally Portugal, suffered significant loss of overseas territory for its brief involvement. The basis for the American independence movement and also for a popular uprising in France was also being laid.

Fig 8: - Europe in 1815

North America

By the 1760s the British colonies in North America had achieved a good degree of self-sufficiency and with a substantial population of around 1.6 million. There was no direct taxation from Britain, colonists enjoyed freedom of religion and, though each colony had an appointed Governor, self-rule was more the order of the day through local assemblies ("Burgesses"). There were tensions, however: a general dislike of aristocratic control from afar; limitation on any expansion westwards; and a British prohibition on trade with other nations, exacerbated by an awareness of scandals within the East India Company. Matters came to a head when Britain's need for funds saw a series of new taxes being imposed on the colonies, mainly through Import Duties, but also directly through a "Stamp Act" requiring all paper used in the colonies for such uses as legal documents and newspapers to employ only British product containing a revenue stamp. Whilst relatively quickly repealed, that latter Act provided a focus for discontent and a ban on trade with Britain with a catch cry of "no taxation without representation" – a fairly impractical demand but a useful rallying slogan. Active hostilities broke out in 1775 and twelve months later a Continental Congress of the colonies issued a formal Declaration of Independence.

Britain struggled to adequately logistically support its forces in North America and resentment in the colonies grew dramatically when it was learned that they intended using German mercenaries (known as Hessians) against the colonists. Tactical victories were achieved by both sides of the conflict all along the eastern seaboard without a conclusive outcome being in sight but then France entered the war in 1778. Her involvement was decisive. Britain's limited naval superiority in the Western Atlantic was largely neutralized and an inability to redeploy troops from a siege at Yorktown (Virginia) in 1781 effectively brought the war to a conclusion. Lengthy negotiations ensued, resulting in the 1783 Treaty of Paris (twenty years after the first Treaty of Paris which had supposedly ended war between Britain and France) recognizing the "United States of America" as a free, sovereign and independent state.

France

By the time of the second Treaty of Paris, France's finances were in a parlous state. The cost of war against Britain, including supporting the American revolution, certainly played a significant part but largely the problem was systemic. Whilst national expenditure approval rested with the monarch, taxation was the province of the Estates General, formed by three separate assemblies of clergy, nobles and commons. The clergy and nobles, however, were exempt from taxation and the Estates General had not sat for over 170 years. Any attempt to increase taxation would have been fraught in those circumstances – and such it turned out to be. Meanwhile the population, now the largest in Europe at around 26 million, was not unmindful of the republican sentiments espoused during the American colonies' fight for independence. Moreover, agricultural failures had led to food shortages, unemployment was rife and a general breakdown in law and order loomed.

What ensued were the storming of the Bastille (1789); the formation of a new National Assembly, principally composed of commoners (the Third Estate); the declared intention of producing a new Constitution; and a *"Declaration of the Rights of Man and of the Citizen"*. The Bastille was a particular target for attack because of its perceived symbolic association with an oppressive monarchy and more practically because it held the local gunpowder supplies. Ultimately acceding to popular demands, the king acknowledged the Declaration and apparently accepted a new state of "constitutional monarchy". Whilst that introduced a period of relative peace, political debate and division continued ferociously whilst rural poverty, confiscation of church property and dissolution of monasteries generated general unease. France was declared a republic in 1792 and many members of the nobility, including senior army officers, who had not already done so, fled overseas.

Being under effective house arrest in the Tuileries Palace (Paris), Louis XVI sought to escape in disguise but was identified and arrested. He was executed in 1793 and Queen Marie Antoinette (she of the probably libelous *"let them eat cake"* fame) followed him to the guillotine nine months later. A "reign of terror" then prevailed across France, with the execution of any perceived opponents to the revolution – numbering in the tens of thousands – many without trial. Meanwhile the National Convention, as the legislative body was then known, had not been idle: the army was being reorganized; conscription was introduced and war was declared on Austria, to be followed later by the Dutch Republic, Prussia, Britain and Spain for good measure. Some idea of the national fervor then being drummed up can be gauged from the words of the *Marseillaise*, composed in 1792 and then titled *Song of War for the Rhine Army.* Subsequently adopted as the French national anthem the song is a call to arms against *"...ferocious soldiers (who) ... are coming to cut the throats of your sons and women"*.

The ensuing conflict initially saw mixed French success but with a growing and improving army of some one million troops, France was seemingly becoming unstoppable in Europe, led by a rising General Napoleon Bonaparte. Holland, Prussia and Spain, closely followed by Austria, all sued for peace. That left Britain whose strength lay mainly in her naval capability. To protect French trade and limit British access to India, Napoleon invaded and took Egypt in 1798. In a subsequent naval engagement, however, a battle subsequently known as the Battle of the Nile, the British under Horatio Nelson effectively destroyed the supporting French fleet and Napoleon was forced to withdraw. On his return to Paris, already by this time a national hero, he abolished the ruling executive and was declared Consul, effectively as dictator. He reinforced that position with the defeat of Austrian forces, expelling them from northern Italy and successfully invaded Bavaria (SE Germany). A short-lived peace with Britain was then negotiated in 1802 - the *"Treaty of Amiens"* - by which Britain, in pursuit of improved European trade, formally recognized the Republic of France. The country had thus replaced absolute monarchy with absolute dictatorship but regained national pride, respect and a degree of internal stability.

Peace between France and Britain was a temporary interlude. Having conquered or subjugated most of mainland Europe, Napoleon was still opposed by Britain and there began a period of economic warfare whereby trade, both between the two countries and with their respective allies was banned. British trade with Europe still flowed, albeit reduced, through her ally Portugal and also through Russia. French invasions of Portugal in 1807 and Russia in 1812 to stop that were resounding failures and French weaknesses thereby exposed encouraged other European powers to re-ignite the fight for their own independence. Europe once again became a wide-ranging battleground, a situation which prevailed until Napoleon was finally defeated by a combined British and Prussian force at the Battle of Waterloo (near Brussels) in 1815.

A separate victim of the European war was the fledgling United States as trade embargoes devastated their cotton and tobacco exports whilst their shipping was being subjected to arbitrary searches and seizures by the Royal Navy. The USA formally declared war on Britain in 1812 and threatened British possessions in what subsequently became Canada. The ensuing conflict lasted less than three years and was an exercise in futility. Britain managed to take Washington and burn the White House and Capitol Building but at the other end of the country were defeated in an attempt to take New Orleans. Losses to injury and disease added to both lives lost in battle and overall financial losses on both sides and the Treaty of Ghent (Belgium) that brought peace saw no substantive change in territories or status.

<u>**Industrialization**</u>

Britain at the time was much in need of export markets: it was progressively industrializing and producing more goods faster. Land reform and improved livestock were playing their part in feeding a growing population but probably the most significant element of progress during the period was the use of coal. When applied to firing steel mills and generating steam for newly developed engines it was transforming British society and that country was then producing far more coal than the rest of the world put together. Steam engines, initially developed for pumping water from mines, gradually found applications in road vehicles, railway engines, steamships and mechanized wool and cotton mills. The increased availability of steel similarly enabled the fabrication of structures and equipment previously impractical. The country's production of textiles and iron increased such that by the end of this period in 1850 it constituted about half of the entire world supply. This being despite this relatively tiny nation having less than two percent of the world's population.

The preceding achievements were enabled by mass production and mechanization (industrialization if you will), combined with having the world's most powerful navy that safeguarded its overseas markets. That process was not without its domestic social upheaval. People needed to move to where the work was, and that was in the increasingly prevalent factories in urban centres at the expense of cottage industries, agriculture and rural life generally. It was also increasingly the case that working conditions in those productive mines, mills and factories were, by any standards, abysmal. Very long hours of labour and oppressive management in circumstances of poor food and low pay led to disease and virtual servitude with little recourse.

The British Parliament, composed primarily of wealthy landowners, did nothing to help the working class and went so far in 1799, doubtless conscious of the revolutionary scene in France, as to introduce a *"Combination Act"* which prohibited workers from combining to object to their conditions or forming any sort of union. Though repealed in 1824, that Act typified the self-serving attitude of Parliament as it then was and the need for reform. It is perhaps unsurprising that when a Reform Bill was finally introduced but then thrown out by the House of Lords, there was rioting in the streets. It would, however, take more than another century before universal suffrage was achieved and working people could thus have some say in their treatment.

Industrialization in USA

After declaring independence in 1776, the USA was fully occupied with its conflict with Britain for the next seven years but afterwards still constituted little more than thirteen colonial outposts on the eastern edge of the continent. The economy was in a bad way and most of the population were farmers who consumed what they produced, although coffee, sugar and tobacco were still being exported, mainly to German ports. The population was neither ignorant nor blind to foreign developments, however, with immigration, overseas agents and an active press keeping the country well informed of industrial progress in Britain. What followed was perhaps the world's first acknowledged case of state sponsored industrial espionage whereby British citizens with access to technological secrets were actively encouraged, in some cases sponsored, to emigrate to the USA. A *Congressional Patent Act* enacted in 1793 then provided US patent protection to resulting pirated technology.

One of the first stolen British designs set to work was that for a water-powered textile mill. By 1810 there were something like eighty-five cotton spinning mills in use or under construction and in 1815 the complete design for an integrated spinning and weaving factory was smuggled into the country. Industrialization was thus well underway in the US by the 1830s but still reliant in the import of heavy machinery such as railway locomotives. In 1831 the design of an imported British locomotive (the "John Bull") was copied during re-assembly and manufactured locally. Within a further six years three-quarters of all railway locomotives in the USA were being made in country. Industrialization was becoming entrenched.

<u>**Possession and Dispossession**</u>

Whilst efforts to achieve independence, most notably amongst Europeans, were a mark of the Age, such independence elsewhere was under threat, also mainly from Europeans.

At the opposite side of the globe in 1788, in a relatively remote and undeveloped cove on the eastern seaboard of what became **Australia**, over 750 convicts and their Marine minders were being landed to form a new colony. Some descendants of the original aboriginal population would prefer to describe that event as an invasion but, if so, then by any standards it was a relatively benign one. The settlers were under government edict to communicate with, protect and show kindness to the native people with punishments applying to any who harmed them. Nonetheless, the European possession of the land necessarily involved aboriginal dispossession. There were perhaps between 500,000 and 750,000 aboriginals then inhabiting Australia. Whilst not evenly distributed, in a land mass having close to three million square miles, it is clear that the aboriginal population was not crowded and comprised up to three hundred different language groups, mainly living in dispersed family, tribal or 'clan' communities. They were not an "advanced" people in any technological sense.

Overcoming near starvation, infertile land and a thorough lack of agricultural skills, the convict colony expanded throughout the Age, though not without conflict with the native population whose land was being usurped. Inland and coastal exploration progressed relatively rapidly.

Land in New South Wales and Victoria had been found suitable for sheep, cattle and general agriculture with wool becoming a valuable export commodity within a couple of decades. By 1803 the continent had been circumnavigated and before the end of this Age additional colonies had progressively been established in each of what are now modern States – Tasmania (1803), Queensland (1825), Western Australia (1829), Victoria (1834) and South Australia (1836). By 1850 the population of Australia had grown to some 400,000. Free settlers gradually outnumbered transported convicts and the last of the convict ships arrived in New South Wales in 1850 to much local disapproval.

Friction over land ownership between settler and native was continuous, often resulting in outright conflict and unlawful killing. Sporadic, well-meaning and almost certainly misguided efforts at assimilation of aboriginals proved largely fruitless and often left subsequent generations disconnected from their heritage and culture. Discontent over that and land rights continues to this day.

In the **USA** a similar expansion of settlement and consequent native dispossession occurred although on a much larger scale. The native population (wrongly named Indians) at the beginning of the Age (1750) was possibly between three and four million, although subsequent epidemics of smallpox (1780 and 1837) together with a malaria epidemic in 1833 and continual outbreaks of influenza and measles caused massive reductions. Hostilities with the settlers added to the losses and by the end of the Age (1850) the population was significantly below half a million.

Once the US settler community had gained independence it was virtually inevitable that its eyes would turn toward the great open spaces to the west. Opportunity came knocking with the purchase of land from Napoleonic France in 1803 (the *"Louisiana Purchase"*) whereby the country acquired some 530 million acres. Added to that were lands already acquired through war with native tribes (the "Indian Wars") and associated treaties or being acquired through purchases and exchanges that provided for settlement on previously native lands. Ultimately an 1830 *"Indian Removal Act"* provided for the forced removal of native Americans from east of the Mississippi River to federal land further west. This resulted in events such as what became known as the *"Trail of Tears"* whereby some 60,000 members of five notable tribes – progressively, Choctaw, Seminole, Creek, Chickasaw and finally Cherokee – were forced to leave their traditional lands and trek thousands of miles in miserable conditions to federally-assigned land to the west. Unsurprising many died of disease, starvation or exposure along the way.

Toward the end of this Age some extreme elements of US society began to espouse a concept of *"Manifest Destiny"*. This entailed belief in a God-given right to occupy the continent of North America in its entirety and had both racial and religious connotations. Intrinsically the concept regarded native Americans and imported African slaves as inferior savages who became mere impediments to progress. This was by no means a universally held belief within the US but in a society with predominantly Christian (and often Puritan) origins and where only Caucasians seemed to be advancing knowledge and industrialization it might be seen how such a philosophy might take hold. That concept, though then primarily territorial in its ambitions, later occasionally resurfaced in notions of American exceptionalism whereby the US was inherently and nobly different from other nations. Whatever the original rationale for the concept, it then conveniently justified dispossession of native Americans and the enforced acquisition of territory from Mexico.

Overleaf: **Geronimo** [U.S. National Archives, Public Domain]. **Born in 1829 of the Apache tribe, Geronimo became well known for his violent opposition to dispossession of traditional Apache lands. He died, technically as a US prisoner of war, in Oklahoma in 1909.**

<u>China</u>

One country which certainly had no apparent threat to its independence at the beginning of this Age was China. Long-reigning Emperors of the Qing who were both conservative and hard-working had engendered a period of relative stability internally and with successful territorial expansion to some 4.5 million square miles. The country was at its zenith in terms of both size and wealth whilst exports of silk, porcelain, paper, cotton and, most significantly, tea, were ensuring a steady inwards flow of silver. Tensions between the dominant Manchu and Han Chinese remained but were alleviated by a less segregated administrative structure that allowed agriculture to flourish and tax revenues to improve. This happy situation was about to change dramatically.

Foreign traders, mainly from Britain, were permitted to operate only from the southern port of Guangzhou (*Canton*) and were having difficulty achieving a market for their manufactured goods. Unscrupulous traders were, however, finding a ready market for Opium which the British East India Company was shipping from India. The detrimental effect on a progressively increasing population of addicts did not go unnoticed and in 1799 Chinese authorities prohibited the sale of Opium. Four decades of laxity in policing that law came to an end in 1838 when a crackdown resulted in the seizure and destruction of 20,000 chests of imported Opium. That seizure was enormous, constituting over one million kilograms of Opium at a value then in the order of thirty-six million dollars. The British were outraged and demanded compensation – which was unsurprisingly not forthcoming.

At this time the Chinese army had not been involved in significant conflict, other than with minor ethic skirmishes at the edges of the country, for nearly two centuries. They were badly eclipsed in terms of naval and military capability. The British shipped troops from India and used naval superiority – including use of their first iron steam-powered warship *HEIC Nemesis* – to impose an increasingly demanding series of trade-related concessions upon the Chinese. With relatively few casualties the British forces overcame all resistance and progressed up the Pearl River and then the Yangtze River to ultimately threaten Nanking (*Nanjing, E China*). Chinese authorities then saw little option but to agree to demands incorporated in what became the *Treaty of Nanking* signed in 1842 involving the ceding to Britain of Hong Kong; opening four additional trading ports; and paying large sums in "reparations". These measures had dramatic effects on the Chinese domestic economy which, apart from requiring a large outflow of silver, were generating a flood of imported European manufactured goods which in turn disrupted the peasant village industry. Peasant revolts and banditry soon arose and the seeds were sown for far more serious conflict.

**Fig 10: - British East India Company warship
NEMESIS engaging Chinese Junks in First Opium War 7
January 1841.**

*[Original by Thomas Allom, courtesy British Library
and Wikimedia Commons]*

<u>**India**</u>

An uneasy mix of Islam and Hinduism had prevailed in India – then known more readily as Hindustan – for over two centuries at the beginning of the Independence Age. The controlling Islamic Mughal Empire (ethnically Mongols but preferring the title of Chagatai Turks) was, however, in a relatively advanced state of decline and an independence confederacy was making rapid gains. Wars of succession after the last great Mughal ruler Aurangzeb; Persian and Afghan invasions of the Punjab (*now Pakistan*); and the rising power of both Sikhs and the individual Maratha rulers had led to a breakdown in central authority. That void was progressively filled by a confederacy of Maratha rulers which had the aim of self-rule for native Hindus and which, by 1785, constituted an empire that controlled most of the sub-continent.

The Maratha Empire was centrally administered by a council of Ministers with a Prime Minister known as the Peshwa. The sheer expanse of the country, though, together with the diversity and size of its population, then numbering some 125 million, did not allow for any high degree of unified management. Individual provincial and feudal warlords had a good deal of autonomy and operated their own military forces under the overarching policies of the Peshwa and were universally wealthy. Society was highly stratified and whilst the superiority of Muslims as asserted under Moghul rule was diminished, a reinforced caste system, which established status based upon heredity, ensured a rigid social hierarchy. The lower orders were universally poor, literacy levels extremely low and there were certainly few educated women, with no female education facilities until the end of this period. Lower castes were highly vulnerable to famine and one such event in Bengal in 1770 caused the deaths of over a million people.

One unusual fight for independence - from government oppression rather than military control - occurred in 1839 and lasted two decades. This occurred in the southern Indian State of Travancore (*modern Kerda*) and became known as the Channar Revolt. The Nader climber people of the region were considered lower caste (*Avarua*) and women were not permitted to cover their upper bodies. Keeping their breasts thus exposed in public was regarded as a form of respect to higher castes (*Nairs*) and failure to do so incurred a fine known as a "breast tax". This indignity was opposed by missionaries who achieved some concessions on religious grounds for those converting to Christianity but change was fiercely opposed by powerful adherents of the caste system. Violent uprisings ensued and it was not until pressure from the British-appointed Governor of Madras in 1859 that the law was rescinded. In a further more modern oddity all references to the Channar Revolt were removed from Indian secondary education texts in 2016.

Independence was not initially seen as an issue in relation to the arrival of the British East India Company. Having been granted trading rights by Mughal Emperor Jahangir in 1612, the company was, by the beginning of this period, enjoying lucrative business activity based on the ports of Calcutta, Madras, Bombay and Cuddalore (*Tamil Nadu, SE India*). After 1750 it began to expand and from an initial guarding force of a few hundred it grew to having over 65,000 armed troops (*sepoys*) within three decades. With European weaponry and associated professional training, it became the most powerful army in the country. The company was by then fully prepared to exercise its original charter from King Charles II enabling it to independently acquire territory, command troops, form alliances and make war or peace. A series of conflicts and alliances with local Nawabs (semi-autonomous local rulers), the Mahrattas (a separate warrior group), Sikhs and the Peshwa himself grew into a series of three full-scale Anglo-Maratha wars. It was not until 1819 that there was any decisive outcome but a British victory left the East India Company in virtually complete control of the entire sub-continent. Hopes of independence and self-rule for native Hindus were thus placed on indefinite hold.

Fig 11: - A Group of Mahrattas, India, 1818.
(*Anonymous: courtesy Wikimedia Commons*)

INDEPENDENCE AGE – MILESTONES
1750 - 1850

18TH CENTURY

1752 – Lightning conductor for building protection invented (Benjamin Franklin).

1754 – French withdraw from India leaving British in control.

1756 – "Seven Years War" begins: a global conflict between France and Britain.

1763 – Treaty of Paris ends war between France and Britain.

1765 – James Watt develops advanced steam engine based on original 1712 design by Thomas Newcomen.

1770 – World's worst famine (10 million dead) strikes Bengal (India).

James Cook explores East coast of Australia; awarded for beating scurvy.

1771 – US Declaration of Independence (4 July).

1779 – Spain declares war on Britain, allying with France and financially and logistically supporting the American revolution.

1783 – Treaties of Paris and Versailles end the American Revolutionary War and that between Britain, France, Spain and the Dutch Republic.

1787 – British fleet of eleven ships sails for Australia with convicts to establish new settlement, ultimately landing Port Jackson (Sydney) 26 January 1788.

1789 – Storming of the Bastille (Paris).

1792 – France declares Republic, abolishes monarchy (executes King Louis XVI 1793). Declares war on Britain, the Netherlands and Spain the following year.

1796 – French army under Napoleon invades Italy, establishing new Republics.

1797 – British navy mutinies at Spithead and Nore over conditions.

1798 – Napoleon invades Egypt, takes Alexandria and Cairo. British under Nelson destroy his naval support; Napoleon returns to Paris; becomes Dictator in following year.

1800 – Electric battery invented – Alessandro Volta.

19th CENTURY (part 1)

1801 - Tripoli (Barbary coast, N Africa), at war with Sweden, also declares war on USA.

Treaty of Amiens by which Britain acknowledges French Republic.

1803 - Britain declares war on France. Napoleonic wars continue until 1815.

USA purchases Louisiana Territory (828,000 sq miles) from France for $15,000.

1804 –Australian Convict uprising at Castle Hill (New South Wales) – mainly Irish rebels.

1805 - Battle of Trafalgar: 27-strong British fleet under Nelson defeats a 33-strong combined French and Spanish fleet off Cape Trafalgar (SW Spain).

1811 – Widespread independence movements begin in South America. Venezuela, Paraguay, Brazil, Argentina, Chile, Greater Colombia, Mexico, Peru, El Salvador, Honduras, Costa Rica, Guatemala, Panama.

1812 - Napoleon invades Russia: fails with enormous loss of life.

USA declares war on Britain: inconclusive hostilities until 1815 peace treaty.

1815 - Battle of Waterloo: Napoleonic forces defeated; Napoleon exiled.

1818 – First successful blood transfusion (James Blundell).

1821 – Greek war of independence begins (continues to 1829).

1822 – First iron steamship launched ("*Aaron Manly*", Britain).

1824 – Cherokee Nation becomes literate in own syllabary of 85 letters. Own newspaper follows.

1825 – First passenger railway opens: 43km Stockton to Darlington, England.

1827 – Screw propellor designed for ships. Next decade sees inventions flourish, including sewing machine, Faraday's dynamo, contraceptive diaphragm, Braille, Shorthand and Morse Code.

1838 - Dutch (*Voortrekker Boer*) settlers defeat Zulu army over land rights in Natal (S Africa).

1839 - Britain invades Afghanistan to prevent Russian control – defeated whilst withdrawing in 1842.

First Opium war begins – Britain attacks Chinese Qing Dynasty to enforce trade access.

1840 – Treaty of Waitangi (N. New Zealand) between Britain and Maori Chiefs.

1842 – Refrigeration using ammonia pioneered.

Treaty of Nanking (*Nanjing, E China*) ends First Opium war; China cedes Hong Kong.

1843 – First Maori War between New Zealand Maoris and white settlers.

Anglo-French Proclamation of the independence of the Kingdom of Hawaii.

1845 – Famine in Europe kills about two million people: potato crops fail.

1846 – USA invades Mexico: begins US-Mexican war. Ends with Treaty of Guadalupe Hidalgo (1848).

1848 – Gold discovery in California (USA) triggers major "gold rush".

1850 – Taiping Rebellion in China between Han and Qing Dynasty begins world's bloodiest civil war.

TRANSITION AGE 1851 – 1950

Each Age of mankind's progress has incorporated transition in one form or another, although the start and end points from one state to another are mostly imprecise. Equally, the actual transition or transitions involved have often been obscure or involved far more than any simple title or single event might describe, even in retrospect. Such was also the case with this Age wherein the rate of change of matters affecting societies was exponential and the matters themselves widely varied and often dramatic. There are myriads of differences between the start and end of this Age that Wiser Persons could address (and mostly have!). One that partly-wise persons might further consider, though, is that gradual shift toward a world view of society rather than those purely State-based concerns and activities that have plagued history. That was always going to be a bumpy ride, and so it transpired. But before we become light-hearted in our appraisal of such "bumps" in the progress of humankind, it is worth remembering that each, whether international conflict, civil war, famine or disease, involved the premature and possibly avoidable death of many thousands of our partly-wise brothers and sisters.

China

For China this Age was as dramatic as it was transforming. The period opened with the country being amidst one of mankind's most devastating conflicts in terms of loss of life – the **Taiping Rebellion** – in which some 20-30 million people were killed. The country was in dire straits and with little going for it except size and population (some 350 million in 1850). Opium use, both imported and local production, was rampant; imported manufactured goods and indemnity payments to Britain were devasting the domestic economy. All this was occurring while famine and increasing demands for improved trade access from Western powers were fueling national humiliation and peasant discontent. The Qing authorities did recognize the problems and made some effort – a *"Self-Strengthening Movement"* – which began in 1861 but achieved only limited success in terms of achieving modernization and institutional reform.

Two failed uprisings (*Guangzhou* in 1895 and *Huizhou* in 1900) and military defeats by Japan (1895) and Russia (1905) exacerbated the national malaise but by then the revolutionary groups had at least refined their objectives, those being nationalism, democracy and family self-sufficiency. A further armed rebellion in 1911 was triggered by nationalization of the railways and enjoyed such success that the Qing Emperor was forced to abdicate within a year. A Nationalist Party (later *Kuomintang, KMT*), formed with the guidance of the charismatic Sun Yat-sen (*Sun Zhongshan*), assumed control of government but repressive measures and conflict with communist elements led to political chaos, not helped by Japanese attempts at subjugation during World War 1. On again -off again cooperation between the Kuomintang and the communist element, formalized in 1921 as the Chinese Communist Party (CCP), ended when all communists were expelled from the KMT in 1927. In response a CCP leader, Mao Zedong (*Mao Tse-tung*), was authorized to form a "Red

Army" to contest KMT power. Mao's Red Army was, however, virtually defeated by 1934 when forced to retreat some 9,000 kilometres to the West then North in a year-long survival exercise that became known as the "Long March".

Ongoing civil war between the CCP and KMT paused under the even more serious threat posed by a Japanese invasion of 1937. That conflict, though often subsumed as part of WW2 was perhaps more accurately known as the Second Sino-Japanese War, lasting until Japan's surrender to US and Allied forces in 1945. A reinvigorated Red Army then pursued hostilities against the KMT with renewed fervor, gaining many soldiers transferring allegiance from the Nationalist army. The KMT accepted defeat in 1949, with the leadership and two million followers fleeing to Taiwan. Mao Tse-tung proclaimed the formation of the People's Republic of China later that year. Mainland China thus completed its transition from imperial dynastic rule that had lasted over two thousand years to a single-party communist State ruled by a People's Congress.

Fig 12 – A rare moment of accord between Mao Tse-Tung of the Red Army and Chiang Kai-shek of the KMT marking the surrender of Japan in 1945. The two parties recommenced hostilities almost immediately thereafter.

(Public domain: original photographer unknown: courtesy Wikimedia Commons)

<u>**Europe**</u>

The years of this Age in Europe were dominated by the lead-up, conduct and aftermath of two World Wars. A key element in the lead-up was the integration of a number of individual States into two discrete entities – a unified Italy and a unified Germany – and in both cases at the expense of the then dominant Habsburg Austria. The combined efforts of King Victor Emmanuel II of Piedmont-Sardinia (*N Italy*) and a revolutionary republican – General Giuseppe Garibaldi – succeeded in variously convincing or forcing the individual Italian States to integrate, with the country being ultimately unified as a kingdom in 1870. The architect of German unification was the then Prussian Prime Minister Otto Von Bismarck, an astute diplomat. Initially focused on forming a confederation of north German States to diminish Austrian influence, he provoked Austrian military retaliation which was defeated in only seven weeks. When Napoleon III, between bouts of womanizing, denied a Prussian the crown of Spain, war with France resulted and again saw an early Prussian victory. That, together with promises of considerable autonomy, convinced the remaining German States and the Proclamation of a German Empire was achieved in 1871.

A second significant element in the lead-up to the two World Wars was the formation of national alliances in an overarching atmosphere of competition and suspicion. Much rested at the door of the physically (and possibly mentally) impaired German Kaiser Wilhelm II who abandoned Bismarck's quiet diplomacy and initiated aggressive naval and colonial expansion. German alliances with Austria-Hungary and Italy were retained but that triggered a compensating alliance between Britain, France and Russia. Tensions rose steadily in the early years of the new century, especially over that pot-mess of nations collectively known by Wiser Persons as "the Balkans". There is no such geographically defined area, but what is generally meant is that area of South-eastern Europe bounded roughly by the Mediterranean in the South, Romania to the North, the Black Sea to the East and the Adriatic to the West. Ethnic tensions there erupted in 1912 in a series of conflicts that lasted two years. The end result was a loss of over 100,000 lives; a mass exodus of Turks from the region; the Ottoman Empire lost most of its European territory; Greece expanded; and ethnic tensions remained.

In 1914 a Serb nationalist assassinated Austrian archduke Franz Ferdinand and his wife. Austria-Hungary blamed Serbia and declared war. Serbia's ally Russia mobilized, whilst Germany, fearing an attack from Russia and its allies, conducted a pre-emptive strike against France: WW1 had begun. British and Russian forces counter-attacked, with the former forcing a stalemate in the West but the latter being defeated in East Germany. Attempts to open a supply route to Russia through the Dardanelles (*W. Turkey*) failed when British and Commonwealth forces were defeated by the Turks at Gallipoli. Italy joined the war in 1915 but, contrary to its earlier alliance, on the side of Britain. It suffered enormous casualties in consequence and was ultimately defeated by Austria-Hungary in 1917. That same year accumulated losses and internal revolution caused Russia to withdraw from the conflict, although the British-French alliance was then bolstered by the USA which, despite significant domestic opposition, declared war on Germany. Both militarily and with mutinies and desertions in its forces, Germany was effectively defeated by November 1918 when an armistice was agreed. A formal end to the war took until June 1919 to achieve with the *Treaty of Versailles*.

Neither the USA nor China signed or ratified the Treaty of Versailles and with 440 clauses it resembled in many respects the theoretical camel designed by committee. Patently bitter about its provisions and their acceptance (albeit under threat of immediate attack) were the people of Germany. Disarmament provisions, loss of overseas territories and payment of reparations amounting to over $US400 billion in today's money were widely seen as unreasonable. Elements of potential long-term good included establishment of the League of Nations, an International Court of Justice and an International Labour Organization. Over the next two decades, though, a potent mixture of economic instability, unemployment, malnutrition and fear of Communism led to a rise in far-right nationalist extremism that became better known as fascism. Benito Mussolini's fascist successes in Italy and Francisco Franco's similar success in Spain were mirrored in Germany with electoral victories by Adolf Hitler's National German Socialist Workers (Nazi) Party.

Hitler became chancellor of Germany in 1933 and immediately began dismantling democratic arrangements. Under an *"Enabling Act"* that gave him autocratic power he promptly banned opposition political parties, annexed Austria and seized Sudetenland (part of Czechoslovakia).

Poland came next, was quickly defeated, and under a pact with Russia was split between Germany in the West and Russia in the East. Apparently unexpected by Hitler was the consequent declaration of war in September 1939 by Britain and France which each had treaties with Poland. WW2 had begun. German forces were fully prepared, however, and quickly overran Belgium, the Netherlands and France, whilst preparing to invade Britain. Hitler's primary target, however, and despite a mutual non-aggression pact, was Russia. On 22 June 1941 he declared that country, to be the source of a world conspiracy of "Jews, democrats and Bolshevists", fostered by the English, to encircle and destroy the new German "socialist order". German forces invaded Russia that same day in what may have been Hitler's greatest strategic mistake. Those forces were ultimately stalled at Stalingrad in 1943 and with added support from the USA which had entered the war in December 1941, the tide was also turning elsewhere. In 1944 the western allies invaded occupied France from Britain, whilst Russian forces advanced steadily from the East. Germany surrendered in May 1945 before which Hitler committed suicide.

No brief synopsis of WW2 can adequately encapsulate the scale, intensity and horror of that conflict, including the mass murder of millions of innocent Jews. Suffice it to say that, of Germany's key allies, Italy surrendered in late 1943 but Japan fought on in what some have regarded as a separate Pacific War until September 1945.

Fig 13: – It is often the innocent that suffer: WW2 image of a Nazi round-up of civilians, mainly Jews, from the Warsaw ghetto. (*Source unknown, courtesy Creative Commons Deed CCO*)

USA

In 1850 the USA was essentially a developing country inhabiting a very large area with a population of only 23 million. Wagon trains were still heading to a poorly explored West and whilst some were rushing to the recently discovered goldfields in California, ranchers and farmers were only just beginning to settle the Great Plains in the centre of the country. Hostile tribes, of which the Apache and Sioux were notably aggressive, fiercely resisted new settlement and there was much loss of life on both sides, mostly in a thirty-year period between 1860 and 1890. The start of that period coincided with an outbreak of civil war between Northern (*"Union"*) states and the eleven Southern *("Confederate")* states that seceded due mainly in resistance to the abolition of slavery. This latter conflict was of much shorter duration (1861-1865) than the so-called "Indian Wars" but caused a substantially greater loss of life – some 600,000 lives. Initially the Confederate forces demonstrated superior military ability and achieved much success but were eventually worn down by the sheer weight of resources that the Union forces could draw upon. After a major defeat at Gettysburg (*Pennsylvania*) the confederacy surrendered in April 1865.

The reunited USA saw a surge in immigration in the latter part of the 19th Century, mainly from Europe but from as far afield as China (the *"Coolie"* trade). With that came a similar increase in industrial production – it overtook Britain in that regard by the early 1900s – and an associated rise in consumerism. A period of what some critics would deride as hedonism was evident in the early 20th Century ("the

Roaring Twenties") but that came to a nasty end with a stock market crash of 1929 and a desperate time of widespread unemployment and soup kitchens. Government efforts to ameliorate the situation with a program of public works were slow to take effect and general poverty was made worse by a drought in the Great Plains in the mid-1930s. Light at the end of tunnel arose with the demand for war materials for Britain but was dimmed by a prohibition on sales to "foreign nations at war" (*Neutrality Acts 1935, 1937 and 1939*). There was, however, a "cash and carry" clause that permitted sales for cash at Presidential discretion and this took effect. Britain paid in gold bullion for arms and associated supplies until late 1940 by which time Britain was close to bankruptcy and could no longer pay. A "lend-lease" arrangement was then negotiated on favorable terms to Britain, although a major technology transfer regime was also initiated in which USA gained British technologies such as that for jet engines, radar, gyros and plastic explosives, including the scientific basis for a nuclear bomb (*Frisch-Peierls Memorandum 1940*).

Japanese forces attacked the USA, notably at Pearl Harbor (*Hawaii*), on 7 December 1941. Having already occupied much of China, Japan's leadership was intent on expanding to form a "Greater East Asia Co-Prosperity Sphere'. Combined with a realization that the oil and steel embargo applied by the UK and USA followed by the Netherlands in July 1941 would cripple their economic and military capabilities, their invasion of Thailand and simultaneous attacks on Malaya, Singapore, Hong Kong, Hawaii, Wake Island, Guam and the Philippines were, in hindsight, quite predictable. The attacks did, however, take US forces by surprise, especially as there had been no prior declaration of war. The USA responded by formally declaring war on Japan on 8 December 1941 and on Germany three days later. The conduct of the war is canvassed extensively elsewhere but in terms of the Pacific theatre a program of aggressive "island hopping", fire-bombing of Japanese cities and, ultimately, the dropping of atomic bombs on Hiroshima and Nagasaki (*W and SW Japan*) forced the Japanese to surrender, which they did formally on 2 September 1942, some four months after that of Germany.

By the end of this Age, the USA was a thoroughly transformed nation from that at the beginning. With a population in 1950 in the order of 150 million, the country was unified, militarily powerful, with a strong economy, a highly industrialized production capability and a presence on the world stage eclipsed by no other.

Africa

Africa in 1850 was still largely the unknown continent (except to the Africans themselves of course). There were European trading ports scattered around the periphery but internally, areas such as the Congo, though covering some 4 million square kilometres, constituted a blank spot in terms of external awareness. What was known, or at least suspected, was the presence of substantial resources, including rubber, ivory, gold, timber and (at that stage), slaves. At the instigation of the ever-active German diplomat Bismarck a conference of interested powers – some fourteen countries – was convened in Berlin in 1884 to resolve competing interests there. No Africans were involved. The outcome was that the African continent was effectively divided between the European powers, albeit with conditions. Those included the end of slavery; a principle of "effective occupation" that required proper administration and policing; and free trade along the Congo and Niger rivers. In very broad terms Britain was accorded colonial rights in the North-East and South, France in the North-West, Belgium centrally and remaining states (Germany, Spain, Portugal and Italy) in various enclaves around the coast.

It would be futile to attempt any common picture of the impact and conditions prevailing during European colonization of this vast African continent. The situation in the Pharaonic nation of Egypt in the north and that of tribal southern Africa, despite homo erectus having lived in that latter region for millennia, were entirely different. In most areas, though, there was a common colonial priority – profit – and much of the development was driven by commercial interests. Rarely, if ever in its fullest sense, did colonists integrate with the local population. Their presence was occasionally welcomed, sometimes merely tolerated and very often violently opposed. The list of wars and conflicts in Africa over this period is daunting, not counting the better-known Zulu and Boer wars in South Africa (see timeline). Development and external trade flourished, although at the cost of great disruption to self-sufficient tribal and agricultural communities, and towns and cities grew markedly. Increasingly educated urban populations became less tolerant of colonial rule and, especially after the European powers were weakened by the two World

Wars, demands for national independence were becoming stronger as this period ended.

Fig 14: - Boers at Spion Kop (*SE South Africa*), 1900

(Project_Gutenberg_eText_16462 Public Domain, https://commons.wikimedia.org/w/index.php?curid=4395 40)

<u>India</u>

The dominant authority in India at the beginning of this Age was still the British East India Company which exerted its control over a diverse population of some 200 million. Despite the company's overriding priority being commercial exploitation of resources such as cotton, spices, silk and tea, it did introduce stability and reasonable governance to the country. Its approach was, however, heavy-handed and disquiet accumulated over a range of issues including taxation, inequality, social reforms and their attitude of superiority. In 1857 a rumour over use of animal fats on rifle cartridges – which would have been offensive to Hindus if beef and to Muslims if pork – apparently triggered a localized mutiny which spread into a general uprising. Fighting was vicious, including the sacking of Delhi, and was only suppressed in mid-1858. Governance was removed from the company in consequence and assumed directly by the British monarchy.

Subsequent British rule over India paid more attention to treaties with the semi-autonomous "princely" (or native) states, of which there were between five and six hundred, and avoided intervention in existing social norms. Toward the end of the 19th Century an educated middle class was making its presence felt and an "Indian National Congress" was formed in 1885 comprising a mix of nationalists and social reformers (or sometimes both). An awareness that arrangements with Britain fell short of being equal grew significantly after the turn of the century and independence became a key issue. Fostered by notables such as Mahatma Gandhi, a program of civil disobedience and/or "non-violent resistance" to British rule became widespread, including boycotts of foreign-made goods. After the two World Wars, in which India provided substantial forces (without consultation with Indian leaders) and suffered over a million casualties, the case for independence became unarguable except for concerns over the prospect of domestic Muslim and Hindu conflict. Ultimately, British rule was ended in 1947 but the process included a partition of what became the two independent States of mainly Hindu India and mainly Muslim Pakistan. This partition was never going to be without difficulty and the Maharaja of Jammu and Kashmir in the North pragmatically declined to affiliate with either new country. When tensions grew, he made a last-minute accession to India but Pakistani tribal forces invaded and war between India and Pakistan began. The area of Kashmir has continued as a source of conflict.

Immediately to the East, Burmese expansion had resulted in both military operations and refugees spilling across an imprecisely demarcated border and in 1853 the British East India Company had the area of southern Burma annexed and renamed Lower Burma. Subsequent concerns over Burmese affiliations developing with the French led to war, which Britain declared on rather nebulous grounds. Having succeeded in defeating Burmese forces, Britain then annexed the whole of Burma as a province of India. This situation prevailed until 1937 when the country became a separate British colony, ultimately achieving independence in 1948 as the nation now known as Myanmar.

Fig 15: – The slight but highly influential figure of Mahatma Gandhi, India 1930.

(Unknown photographer, Public Domain: courtesy Wikimedia Creative Commons)

<u>**Australasia**</u>

In 1850 the population of **Australia** was around 400,000: by 1950 it had risen to more than eight million, almost entirely through immigration. A British Act - *the "Australian Colonies Government Act"* of 1850 – provided for democratically elected governments in four locations (New South Wales, Victoria, South Australia and Tasmania), each being constitutional monarchies under the British monarch. Within six years secret ballots had been introduced. In the meantime, however, gold had been discovered and, whilst spurring an increase in immigration, also encouraged more exploration of what was a largely unknown and, as it transpired, somewhat barren inland. Population centres remained disbursed around the coastline and communication between them was slow until an overland telegraph was constructed in 1872 spanning some 3,000 kilometres from south to north. It had taken some ten years to construct and complemented an East-West telegraph of a further 3,000 kilometres. Better, faster, shared communications fostered a greater awareness of the country's place in the world and in the 1890s concerns over inefficiencies, defence vulnerability and differing immigration policies between the colonies generated a movement toward a national approach. This wish accelerated after a financial crisis peaking in 1893 whereby banks failed; a serious Depression arose and there was no common national response.

After much debate and a series of referenda, the six self-governing colonies of Australia federated as the Commonwealth of Australia with effect from 1901. The following year the female (non-aboriginal) franchise was enacted and a series of nation building endeavours began. The health of the nation's finances was wildly cyclic throughout this Age. Historically reliant on wool as an export commodity, wheat and wine growing rapidly caught up but manufacturing was slow until the impetus of the two World Wars, between which a second major economic collapse again resulted in a severe Depression. National support for Britain in WW1 was enthusiastic and some 320,000 soldiers served overseas. Losses, such as at Gallipoli (Turkey) and in France and Belgium were substantial and, overall, some 60,000 lives were lost with more than twice that number badly injured. Additionally, more than half that number of Australian lives were lost during WW2. By 1950 the nation was politically more mature with a broader economic base and an independent foreign policy leaning more towards the USA than Britain.

New Zealand (*"Aotearoa"*) followed a similar colonization path as Australia although, despite a formal treaty between the government and indigenous (Maori) leaders (*1840 Treaty of Waitangi*), conflict between colonists and indigenous people was both more concentrated and more ferocious. Wars over disputed land acquisition lasted intermittently for some twenty-seven years until 1872 and at one stage involved up to 18,000 British troops. By then the country was well and truly independent, having been established as a parliamentary democracy which took practical effect in 1854 (*New Zealand Constitution Act 1852*). After 1871 the nation experienced its own "migration Age" (the second if one counts the Polynesian settlement of the 14th Century), mainly from Ireland and Britain under "assisted passage" schemes. Unfortunately, economic depression soon took hold and the wool-based economy suffered, having lost the earlier benefits of gold discoveries. The saving grace was the introduction of refrigerated transport which, with modernized international shipping, enabled a growing export industry in beef, lamb and dairy products which the country could produce in excess.

The two World Wars saw a significant military contribution to the British war effort from a relatively low population base – some 100,000 troops in WW1 and 135,000 in WW2. Fighting in concert with Australians under the "ANZAC" (Australian New Zealand Army Corps) banner substantial losses, including those at Gallipoli, forged a strong trans-Tasman bond. The nation itself was also subtly transformed by the war years: urbanization, unionization and welfare became key policy issues and the status of women improved. By 1950 the population of New Zealand was some two million, enjoying a sound economy and leaning once more to relatively conservative policies.

Internationalism

There is nothing wrong with nationalism: indeed, pride in one's country is a noble and wholly praiseworthy characteristic. It is all too easy, though, for us partly-wise humans to take that sentiment to extremes ("*ultranationalism*") whilst forgetting, or deliberately ignoring, the fact that the sentiments of other nationalities have similar standing. Such thinking leads to fascism and the rise of dictators. Such concerns, together with the widespread horror of the carnage of WW1, led to the birth of the League of Nations in 1920. That august organization patently failed, however, in its aim of using dispute settlement measures to avoid future wars. Amidst the ashes of WW2, therefore, the United Nations (UN) came into being as its successor. Taking a broader view of the world, its objectives were *to maintain international order peace and security, to develop friendly relations among nations and to cooperate in solving international economic, social, cultural and humanitarian problems.* The UN achieved some successes (for example in Cambodia, El Salvador, Mozambique and Namibia etc) but also some failures such as in Somalia and Rwanda. It has also spawned a number of internationally valued subsidiary organizations such as the World Health Organization (WHO) and in 1948 sponsored the Universal Declaration of Human Rights. The thirty articles of that Declaration encapsulated the desires of much of the human race, including rights to freedom of speech and belief and also from fear and want.

In 1901 the first Nobel Peace Prize was awarded to a Swiss businessman whose efforts have often gone unremarked upon. Those efforts led directly to the establishment of the Red Cross in Geneva in 1863 and the Geneva Convention the following year on conduct in armed conflict (subsequently updated in 1949). Both those endeavours subsequently contributed greatly to alleviating the worst excesses of conflict.

Definitely not confined to any national boundaries was, over this and prior Ages, the plight of half our world's population – women. Women's suffrage – the right to vote in elections – was a prominent issue in this Age and some limited progress was made. New Zealand first introduced female voting rights in 1893, followed by Australia the following year (for non-aboriginal women) and Norway in 1913. An International Alliance of Women was founded in 1904 as a non-government organization to promote women's rights and gender equality but success was similarly limited. The transition to fully equal rights regardless of gender was drastically incomplete at the end of this Age. Issues relating to holding public office, freedom from sexual violence, work, pay, property ownership and education remained outstanding.

TRANSITION AGE – MILESTONES 1851 - 1950

19TH CENTURY (part 2)

1853 – USA threaten Japanese capital Edo to force trade access.

Crimean War begins: Britain, France and Ottoman Empire versus Russia, caused by a mixture of a wish for Russian containment and support for Christians in Palestine. Consequent loss of life amounted to some 250,000.

1856 – Crimean War ends with Treaty of Paris; Russian warships excluded from Black Sea.

1857 – Indian Rebellion – a combination of army (*'Sepoy'*) mutiny and civilian rebellion against the British East India Company mainly over religious and cultural issues. After suppression the 1858 UK *'Government of India Act'* provided for the dissolution of the Company and for UK Government control of India.

1861 – United States (USA) civil war. Hostilities arising over attempted secession from the Union by mainly southern (*'Confederate'*) states over the key issue of slavery. Militarily defeated, the confederacy collapsed in 1865 with slavery in the USA being abolished.

1862 – Muslim (Tungan) Rebellion in NW China. An uprising of the Muslim Hui against the ethnic Han Chinese and Manchu Qing associated with both a breakdown in social order and racial and religious differences. Mostly suppressed by 1873 except for Xinjiang region which took another five years.

1863 – Cambodia becomes French Protectorate as part of French Indochina.

1864 – Chincha Islands War involving apparent Spanish attempts to reassert influence in its former South American colonies (Peru, Chile, Ecuador, Bolivia). It began with Spanish occupation of the island of Chincha and ended in failure two years later.

1867 – USA purchases Alaska from Russia.

1875 – Decade-long famine in India kills 26 million people: shorter famine in China a year later takes another 13 million lives.

1879 – Anglo-Zulu war in S Africa: deliberately provoked to neutralize Zulu military power. Despite significant losses the British achieved their aim within the year and the Zulu Kingdom was broken up into thirteen individual chiefdoms.

1880 – First Boer War: a sporadic uprising of Dutch/Huguenot settlers in the Transvaal (S Africa) against British rule. Outcome was an 1881 treaty acknowledging Boer autonomy as a tributary State of the British.

1882 – British invasion and occupation of Egypt, then a vassal State of the Ottoman Empire. Bankruptcy and an attempted (and ongoing) coup the previous year generated instability threatening British investments (especially the Suez Canal) and trade. A substantial British naval and land force overcame resistance relatively quickly and Egypt remained occupied until 1936.

1883 – Island of Krakatoa (Indonesia) erupts. N. hemisphere skies darkened.

1884 – Sino-French War – an undeclared conflict over French control of Vietnam which lasted eight months.

French success at sea and Chinese success on land resulted in a virtually fruitless outcome for both sides.

1893 – US forces overthrow Hawaiian monarchy. A force of US marines provides support for a coup orchestrated by US residents. The islands' strategic significance (e.g., Pearl Harbor) outweighs moral and legal concerns and Hawaii is formally annexed by the US five years later.

1894 – Japan and China declare war over Korea, then a tributary state of China. Japanese forces successful; China recognizes Korean independence and cedes Taiwan to Japan in 1895.

1897 – Greco-Turkish War. Fought over Crete which was a vassal State of the Ottoman Empire but had a majority Greek population. The outcome was an ignominious loss by Greece but increased autonomy for Crete.

1898 – Spanish-American War. A four-month conflict between the US and Spain over control of Cuba which was fighting for independence. Peace terms left a victorious US with control of Cuba, the Philippines, Guam and Puerto Rico.

1899 – Boxer Rebellion (N. China). An uprising by a militia group named Boxers - named for their practice of martial arts (Chinese boxing) - who had become violently opposed to foreigners and especially Christians.

1900 – Western alliance of eight nations defeats Chinese imperial army in process of relieving a Boxer siege of Westerners and Christians in Beijing.

20th CENTURY (part 1)

1901 – Commonwealth of Australia formed as six British colonies federate.

1903 – First powered flight by manned aircraft.

1905 – First Russian Revolution. Following a humiliating naval and military defeat by Japan in an attempt to gain an ice-free Pacific port, impoverished peasants, workers and some military rose in protest at conditions. The uprising was suppressed but forced the introduction of a range of personal freedoms.

1908 – Tunguska Event: 12 megaton air-burst of meteorite above Siberia.

1911 – Xinhai Revolution ends Chinese Manchu Qing dynasty and imperial rule.

1914 – World War 1. Begun after a 19-year-old Bosnia Serb, a Yugoslav nationalist, assassinated the Austro-Hungarian heir for which Austria-Hungary held Serbia responsible and declared war. Russia responded in Serbia's defence which brought an alliance of Russia, Britain and France into conflict with the existing alliance of Germany, Italy and Austria-Hungary. British-related nations – Australia, Canada, New Zealand, South Africa and India – provided forces in support of Britain; Italy later shifted allegiance by declaring war on Germany and the USA joined the allied powers in 1917. An armistice ended hostilities in November 1918 although a formal peace treaty – the Treaty of Versailles – was not signed until July 1919.

1917 – Russian 'October Revolution' leads to civil war and end of Russian Empire.

1918 – Influenza pandemic – possibly the world's deadliest – kills up to 50 million.

1919 – Treaty of Versailles, calling for Germany to disarm and make reparations, formalizes the end of WW1.

1920 – League of Nations formed in Geneva (Switzerland) to promote world peace and diplomacy.

1927 – Chinese civil war: Nationalists (Kuomintang) versus Communist Party (CCP).

1928 – Kellogg-Brand Pact: "The General Treaty for Renunciation of War as an Instrument of National Policy" ratified by 63 countries.

1929 – Great Depression: a deep and widespread international economic depression lasting through much of the 1930s. High unemployment affected both secondary and rural industries as trade collapsed causing much impoverishment and civil unrest.

1938 – Time Magazine declares Adolf Hitler "Man of the Year" (but claimed not to be in praise).

1939 – World War 2 (WW2). Global war lasting to 1945 and actively involving over thirty nations with a death toll in the order of 70-80 million. Initiated when Germany invaded Poland, in response to which Britain and France declared war on Germany. Italy and Japan (which was already at war with China) allied with Germany, becoming known as the Axis powers whilst British Commonwealth countries allied with Britain. Further expansion occurred in 1941 when Germany invaded Russia and Japan attacked the USA thus bringing both those attacked nations into the war against the Axis.

1945 – WW2 ends with the unconditional surrender of Germany and then by Japan, the latter after two nuclear bombs were detonated over Hiroshima and Nagasaki.
United Nations formed.

1946 – Italy becomes a Republic.

1947 – Militant Jewish nationalists step up terrorist bombings and murders of British and Arabs in Palestine.

1948 – British mandate for control of Palestine ends: State of Israel proclaimed. Arab-Israeli War results: Egypt, Jordan, Iraq, Syria and Lebanon attack Israel. Israeli victory cemented territorial expansion by armistice agreements in 1949.

Korea is geographically split between north (Democratic Peoples' Republic of Korea) and south (Republic of Korea), respectively under Soviet Union and USA control.

Universal Declaration of Human Rights adopted.

1950 – Korean War. North Korea invades South Korea in attempted reunification. Initial success thwarted by US counterattacks until China's intervention resulted in stalemate. An armistice in 1953 brought a cessation of active hostilities but a state of war between North and South continues to the present.

Fig 16: - D-Day Landings Normandy (France) 6 June 1944

(Courtesy Wikimedia Commons)

Fig 17: - Nuclear bomb detonations over Hiroshima (L) and Nagasaki (R) 6&9 Aug 1945
(Courtesy Wikimedia Commons)

THE MODERN AGE: 1951 – PRESENT

In the Medieval or earlier Ages, the average citizen rarely cared about who their nation's leaders were nor what they were doing and to whom. Village life simply went on as usual. In this highly interlinked modern world that is no longer the case. Whilst every Age of mankind's journey has involved change of one kind or another, what marks the Modern Age is the <u>rate</u> of such change. Hardly a month has passed when there has not been some form of change, whether that be a new discovery or an innovative manner of communicating or doing business. In the arena of world politics (a word derived from the Greek for *"affairs of the cities"*) changes have been dramatic. At the beginning of this Age it was becoming increasingly evident that international power was steadily concentrating in three nuclear-armed "superpowers" – China, USA and Russia. What follows is a summary of relatively recent events that brought those nations to their present position.

<u>CHINA</u>

With the Kuomintang safely out of the way in Taiwan, Mao Zedong was uninhibited – and ruthless - in his pursuit of agrarian reforms which, by distributing land amongst the peasants, was showing signs of success. The Korean War, in which China engineered a large-scale surprise attack on the UN forces, was a major distraction. Equally, the cost, combined with the consequences of US economic sanctions and debt to the Soviet Union caused economic hardship and Mao launched a "Great Leap Forward" to improve matters. This involved use of the nation's most abundant resource – labour – to increase both agricultural and industrial production in localized collectives. The program, which included restricting the movement of workers, was a failure. Famine resulted and Mao stood down as State Chairman.

By 1966, Mao was re-asserting his leadership and began a major purge of leading officials and introduced a program that became known as the "Cultural Revolution" which included student activists called the "Red Guards", of which there were many millions. The program was nationalistic, violent and denounced virtually anything and anyone deemed conservative, foreign or intellectual. With the country on the verge of civil war, the Red Guards were disbanded after two years but the repressive program continued until Mao died in 1976 and his successor ended the Cultural Revolution. In 1978 Deng Xiaoping, who was less ideological than Mao, assumed supreme leadership and focused on alleviating poverty and introducing economic reform, including an element of free enterprise which came to be known as *capitalism with Chinese characters*. These programs proved highly successful, especially in terms of lifting the majority of the population out of poverty. An incident in Tiananmen Square in 1989, however. whereby unarmed pro-democracy students were brutally and publicly attacked by security forces severely damaged the image of the nation and its leadership.

Toward the end of 2012, Xi Jinping became General Secretary of the Party, then PRC President. He wasted little time in asserting his authority. Focusing initially on countering corruption, establishing internal party discipline and initiating social, economic and military reform, he had an ambitious foreign policy initiative in the "Belt and Road" program. That latter arrangement sought to generate a large international market by use of cultural exchange and major overseas infrastructure investment. Domestically he demonstrated an authoritarian approach, consolidating power to himself and failing to accept dissent, whether that be pro-democracy activism or criticism of the reportedly extensive and arbitrary detention of Uyghur Muslims. Internationally, he has publicly espoused free trade, in line with the country's prior membership of the World Trade Organization, but has shown no hesitancy in imposing trade restrictions on countries (notably USA and Australia) that have questioned China's human rights record or its aggressive attempts to dominate the South China Sea and associated threats to Taiwan.

An ominous health-related development in December 2019 arose when a respiratory disease, later identified as Covid-19 virus, was first detected in Wuhan (*Eastern China*) and began spreading world-wide (and mutating) causing border closures, "lock-downs" and serious, sometimes fatal, illness. By the two-year point (December 2021) the virus had been identified in 222 countries and had infected over 286 million people.

Overall, a nation with the world's largest population and second largest land area was always going to be potentially powerful. In past Ages, though, China had been humbled by Western powers. In the Modern Age, with the world's second largest economy, a powerful military and having a highly nationalistic and authoritarian government, that seems unlikely to be allowed to recur. What alarmed western powers was a perceived increase in the belligerence of China's actions over the area known as the South China Sea and the President's threatening posture towards Taiwan.

RUSSIA

In the preceding half-Century Russia had been through an internal revolution, the ruthless imposition of Marxist-Leninist dogma, two World Wars and the beginning of a "Cold War" stand-off with Western powers. Perhaps unsurprisingly, its economy was in difficulty. Added to that it retained an authoritarian government deeply suspicious of the anti-Communist Western powers. The death of Stalin in 1953 eased some of the worst excesses of internal oppression but not a fierce political antagonism toward full democracy and capitalism. In 1955 the country formed a collective defence arrangement with seven like-minded socialist Republics, known as the Warsaw Pact, to balance the power of the North Atlantic Treaty Organization (NATO) formed six years previously. The following year (1956) an uprising began in Hungary which declared its intention of leaving the Warsaw Pact. That uprising was forcefully suppressed by the Soviets who feared the loss of a buffer between themselves and NATO and the potential formation of a new capitalist State.

The "Cold War" can be broadly regarded as lasting from the end of WW2 in 1945 through to the dissolution of the USSR in 1991. Although outright hostilities were avoided, tensions were often very high. In 1961 Russia decided to close off the Western sectors (USA, UK and

French) of Berlin from the remainder of surrounding Communist East Germany. The resulting Berlin Wall closed off a significant exodus of young intellectuals from the East but proved in the longer term to be detrimental to the international image of Communism and a focus of much Western propaganda. The following year, in response to the deployment by the USA of nuclear ballistic missiles to Italy and Turkey, Russia convinced Cuba to similarly accept a Russian nuclear missile deployment. This being only 140 km off the USA mainland proved unacceptable to the USA government and a blockade of Cuba ensued. The risk of war was high; indeed, a USA U-2 surveillance aircraft was shot down over Cuba; but further conflict was avoided by some very convoluted diplomatic communications. Russia agreed to remove its nuclear weapons from Cuba if the USA would agree to a public statement not to invade Cuba and also remove its nuclear weapons from Turkey and Italy.

In 1978 a coup saw the Communist party take government in Afghanistan. Reforms and repressive policies triggered a revolt by mainly provincial groups and a widespread Islamic insurgency began. With the Afghan government losing control to the mujahideen (Islamic guerrilla fighters), fears of a spreading Islamic movement across Asia and suspicion about a possible change of allegiance by the Afghan leadership, Russia invaded in 1979. As the USA did 21 years later, the country thus became bogged down in a virtually unwinnable guerrilla war for another ten years.

In 1991 a group of senior Soviet officials attempted a coup targeting then President of the Soviet Union Mikhail

Gorbachev and his policies of restructuring (*Perestroika*) and open transparency (*Glasnost*). The coup failed but ultimately triggered declarations of independence by fourteen Soviet Republics, including Russia, and that the Union of the Soviet Socialist Republics no longer existed. Russia thus once more became an independent Republic and, under its new President Boris Yeltsin, abandoned the "Cold War" with the West.

Another region then asserting independence was Chechnya (*SW Russian Federation*), mainly through an Islamic separatist group. Ethnic, especially anti-Russian, tensions had existed in the area since the 16th Century and Russia sought to exert its control by invading in 1994. Two years of bitter conflict proved inconclusive and Russian forces were withdrawn two years later only to re-enter in 1999 with a devastating attack on the capital Grozny. Although the conflict was officially declared over in 2017 and despite having a Russian appointed government, Islamic insurgency has continued sporadically ever since.

Despite its very large land area – the world's largest country – only some 7% of Russia's land is arable. Efforts at transforming the economy to a more capitalistic style market arrangement initially failed and the country suffered a financial crisis in 1998, resulting in devaluation of the Ruble and default on international debt. The economy bounced back relatively quickly, but has remained heavily reliant upon fossil fuel exports (oil, natural gas and coal) which provide over one-third of national income. Domestic income inequality remains an ongoing concern and corruption is reputed to be endemic. Tensions with neighbouring Ukraine – which it has seen as its buffer between itself and NATO – exploded in 2014 when it annexed the Crimean Peninsula by force and actively supported separatist movements in Eastern Ukraine. Though labelled only as a "special military operation", Russia invaded Ukraine in 2022 and active hostilities continued through to 2023 both on the ground and in the air. Sanctions and widespread condemnation resulted, including from the UN, but failed to abate Russian aggression. How the conflict is ultimately resolved, will probably determine the country's future international acceptance.

UNITED STATES OF AMERICA

By the end of the Transition Age, the USA was an internationally powerful nation with a strong and growing domestic economy. At the same time the country was deeply fearful of the spread of communism, engaged in a "cold war" with the Soviet Union and also a very hot one against North Korea. By the time an armistice was achieved in Korea the USA had spent many billions of dollars and incurred a heavy loss of life (some 33,000 lives and over 90,000 wounded). Domestically, anti-communist sentiments ran high with a highly publicized trial and execution of two citizens (Julius and Ethel Rosenberg) for spying for the Soviet Union whilst indiscriminate allegations of communist infiltration were spreading ("*McCarthyism*"). The fervor spread to international affairs when the Central Intelligence Agency (CIA) funded and supported a coup in Guatemala that deposed a democratically elected President accused of communist leanings in favour of a dictator (*Castillo Armas*) who then banned opposition parties.

The 1960s saw the USA in further anti-communist activism abroad, which included two significant failures. A CIA-sponsored attack on communist Cuba at the Bay of Pigs by a group of expatriate civilians was defeated by Cuban forces within two days. Unfortunately, that triggered a Cuban request to the USSR for nuclear missiles to be based there to deter any USA invasion. The subsequent Russian missile deployment was detected and Cuba subjected to a blockade amidst the highest levels of international nuclear tension the world had yet experienced. The peaceful outcome, involving a USA recognition of Cuban sovereignty and a Russian withdrawal of missiles had one beneficial outcome which was the establishment of a hot-line between Washington and Moscow to aid direct resolution of such crises. Two years later, a determination to assist South Vietnam defeat a communist insurgency and attack from the North received impetus from a dubious claim of an attack on a US Destroyer (*USS Maddox*) by North Vietnamese patrol craft. This resulted in the deployment of combat troops to South Vietnam and a naval and air offensive against the North. Amidst growing USA and allied domestic opposition to the war, and despite the application of extensive and sophisticated western firepower, the S. Vietnamese capital Saigon fell to communist forces in 1975. Many men and women died, many others were injured and yet more had their spirit broken in that war and the absence of community support for returned service men and women due to anti-war sentiment made matters worse.

Fig 18: - Vietnam War – Refugees fleeing at Fall of Saigon 1975

(Public Domain by Manhai under CC BY 2.0)

In 1990, over a range of territorial issues, but principally due to its large indebtedness, Iraq invaded and occupied Kuwait. Despite previous support for Iraq – which was largely to counter the potential Islamic threat posed by Iran – US authorities were alarmed that this positioned Iraq to further expand into Saudi Arabia and thus control almost all the Middle East oil supply. With UN and Arab League support, the USA managed to assemble a coalition of 34 other countries to restore Kuwaiti sovereignty. Coalition forces, principally those of the USA, attacked in January 1991 and achieved military victory within two months but decided to minimize casualties by neither seizing Baghdad nor ousting the Iraqi President Saddam Hussein.

Ten years later, on September 11 (9/11 in US abbreviation) 2001, four commercial airliners were hijacked by terrorists. Two were deliberately flown into the World Trade Centre (New York), one into the Pentagon military headquarters (Virginia) and one crashed enroute. Almost 3,000 civilians were killed and many thousands injured. The nation developed an enormous appetite for revenge and *Al Qaeda*, an Islamic group committed to *Jihad* (Holy War) against the USA, was quickly identified as the culprit organization, believed sheltering in Afghanistan. The Afghani government, then another Islamic fundamentalist group – the Taliban *("students")* – refused assistance and the USA, with UK and other support, invaded Afghanistan. Despite early military success, a war of insurgency developed and lasted twenty-one years before a negotiated settlement saw the Taliban regain power.

The country's involvement in the Middle East expanded in 2003 when US Intelligence sources (incorrectly) asserted that Iraq was manufacturing "weapons of mass destruction" (biological and/or nuclear armaments). Joined by the UK, Australia and Poland, the USA invaded Iraq and quickly deposed the ruling, notably despotic, government. As in Afghanistan, an insurgency then developed, which in this case involved armed sectarian groups including *Al Qaeda.* By 2009 sufficient stability had been restored for provincial elections to be held and to install a democratic government. Allied troops (varying coalitions became involved) technically withdrew from Iraq at the end of 2011, although some 20,000 US military remained in the country. Insurgent operations then escalated, including both sectarian units and self-proclaimed Islamic State fighters, such that further US involvement was deemed necessary, principally by the use of air power. Foreign (Western) forces were ultimately not withdrawn from Iraq until early 2020.

With the end of the Soviet era and withdrawal from the Middle East, the US focus shifted more to domestic issues, these being marked by a highly partisan political landscape. After a brief (two-year) recession in 2007/09 the economy recovered gradually but concerns remain over the rising national debt (some $31.5 Trillion - i.e., $31,500,000 Million) remained as of 2023. Domestic social issues have and continue to provide challenges – immigration, homosexual rights, gun control and racism amongst others – which were not helped by a President (DJ Trump) elected in 2017 who became known for intemperate remarks and poor judgement. On the international front, a North

American Free-Trade Agreement was successfully negotiated but attempts to prevent North Korea attain nuclear armaments failed. Relations with China over trade issues and with Russia over interference in Ukraine provide ongoing challenges. USA remains, however, the world's most powerful and influential nation.

International Social Issues

The wellbeing of the human species globally is as varied as their respective climates and geographic whereabouts. Overall, about ten percent of people live in extreme poverty (defined as living on less than $US1.90 per day) which amounts to over 700 million individuals. The spread of the Covid-19 virus is likely to exacerbate that problem. Inequality is a further challenge, especially for women. Whilst advances have been made in the Modern Age, women are severely underrepresented in governments and in some countries two-thirds of the female population are illiterate. Access to education has been a major stumbling block to progress, and this is particularly the case in countries with extremist religious beliefs. Contraception is another religious matter that causes unwanted pregnancies (and prohibits terminations) and some 33,000 girls per day enter (or are forced) into marriage whilst aged under 18.

Of many ongoing concerns, has been an alarming increase in the Modern Age of refugees. World-wide by 2023, there were some 32 million people currently displaced from their native country due to persecution, conflict or violence. That number does not include internally displaced persons.

There have also been remarkably positive achievements in this Age, most notably the development and world-wide distribution of vaccines against Covid-19 in a very short timeframe. Equally, the awareness of changes in Earth's climate and mankind's contribution to that, has received an exponential increase. More recent international climate talks have attracted high-level participation by governments around the world and, whilst still less than ideal, targets of maintaining global temperature rise to less than 2^0C (3.6^0F) are encouraging.

Toward the end of the Age, international tensions continued as a cause for general concern, as did largely related financial difficulties, including high inflation, rising interest rates and energy costs. We (mankind) have managed to place a person, albeit temporarily, on the Moon; maintain a number orbiting 'space stations'; and launch satellites with apparent ease to aid our observation of, and communication on, the planet. The ingenuity involved must surely bode well for ultimate resolution of more of our terrestrial issues.

An abiding issue in the latter part of the century has been the violent dispossession of Palestinians from their land to form a homeland for Jewish people that became the self-declared State of Israel in 1948. Conflict erupted frequently thereafter between Israelis (supported by a strong Zionist lobby in the USA which long-advocated for a Jewish homeland) and various surrounding Arab and Islamic nations and groups.

As of 2023 Earth's human population had risen to a touch over 8 billion (8,000,000,000).

MODERN AGE: MILESTONES 1951 - PRESENT

20TH CENTURY

1952 – Egyptian Revolution begins: military coup removes King Farouk.

1956 – Suez Crisis: Egyptian President Nasser nationalises Suez Canal. Israel, UK, and France invade Egypt: Nasser responds by sinking 40 ships to close canal. US, USSR and domestic pressure force withdrawal. Invasion a military success but a political disaster.

1957 – USSR launches Sputnik 1 artificial satellite beginning "space age".

1961 – Berlin Wall erected to separate East from West Berlin. Touted by Communist East as intended to protect against fascist influences.

Soviet Yuri Gagarin becomes first person in outer space and to orbit Earth aboard Vostok 1.

Bay of Pigs: a failed invasion of Cuba by exiles based in USA which was covertly supported by US agencies. Defeated by Cuban forces within three days.

1962 – Cuban Missile Crisis. Russia agreed to Cuban request to station nuclear missiles there to deter any future invasion by USA. Cuba blockaded in response amidst high tension between USA and USSR. Peaceful outcome resulted in establishment of Moscow-Washington "hot line" to resolve issues.

1964 – US enters Vietnam War to support South Vietnam but fails after 11 years when S. Vietnam surrenders in 1975 to the Communist North.

1966 – Chinese Cultural revolution. Mao Zedong launches purge of intellectuals and perceived enemies of the communist ideology: many are killed or imprisoned.

1967 – Arab-Israel War. Egypt announced closure of Straits of Tiran (separating Gulf of Aqaba and Red Sea) to Israeli shipping. Israel responded by attacking Egypt and allies Syria and Jordan, destroying their military capability in six days.

1969 – Humans walk on the Moon: US Neil Armstrong and Edwin Aldrin land on the moon from NASA's spacecraft Apollo 11.

1972 – Strategic Arms Limitation Treaty. USA and USSR agree to limit number of Intercontinental Ballistic Missiles (ICBM) and Anti-Ballistic Missiles (ABM).

1978 – First "test tube baby" born in UK from artificial insemination.

1979 – USSR Invades Afghanistan to suppress Mujahideen (Islamic rebels supported by USA) and stabilise the country but gets drawn into guerrilla war lasting ten years.

Three Mile Island nuclear incident. Partial meltdown of a nuclear power plant reactor in Pennsylvania USA causing radiation leakage and permanent shutdown.

Iranian Revolution. Armed insurrection topples monarchy and institutes Islamic republic.

1980 – Iran-Iraq War. Iraq invaded Iran to destroy that country's regional dominance and prevent the spread of the Iranian religious movement. Active hostilities lasted eight years and resulted in large mutual loss of life but effective stalemate.

1981 – Human Immunodeficiency Virus (HIV) / acquired immunodeficiency syndrome (AIDS) spreads in sub-Saharan Africa becoming global epidemic.

1986 – Chernobyl nuclear reactor (Pripyat, Ukraine) suffers core meltdown and explosion releasing radioactive contamination over a wide area. Early exclusion zone of 30 km radius established but later expanded and likely to remain inhospitable for 1000s of years.

1989 – Tiananmen Square Incident. Troops and tanks attack unarmed pro-democracy demonstrators in Beijing. Many killed or injured.

1990 – German reunification. German Democratic Republic (East Germany) and Federal Republic of Germany (West Germany) re-unite after progressive collapse of the former. Gulf War. Iraq, heavily in debt, invaded Kuwait and set oilfields on fire sparking international condemnation. Coalition of 35 nations under USA leadership attack to liberate Kuwait and entered Iraq but stopped short of regime change.

1991 – Union of Soviet Socialist Republics (USSR) dissolves, with 14 Republics declaring independence. This also effectively ended the "Cold War" between the Soviets and the West.

1993 – European Union formed from 12 original signatories to the 1992 Maastricht Treaty, removing internal frontiers and pursuing a common foreign and security policy.

1997 – Hong Kong returned to Chinese control after 156 years of British rule.

Kyoto Protocol adopted by 192 parties. Protocol aimed to reduce "greenhouse emissions" based on consensus that human-made carbon dioxide was driving global warming.

2000 – Earth's human population approximately six billion (6,000,000,000).

21st CENTURY

2001 – September 11 terrorist attack in USA and consequent invasion of Afghanistan. Militant Islamic extremists hijack four commercial airliners and conduct destructive suicide attacks on key installations in Washington DC and New York City killing around 3,000 civilians. USA invades Afghanistan in response and to remove control of Afghanistan from the Islamic Taliban and prevent their harbouring al-Qaeda terrorists.

2002 – Bali Bombings. Islamic group Jemaah Islamiyah conduct terrorist bombing of nightclubs at Kuta, Bali Island (*Indonesia*) killing 202 locals and tourists with many more injured. Attacks apparently inspired by al-Qaeda.

2003 – USA invades Iraq over concerns of Weapons of Mass Destruction (WMD) - ultimately proven groundless – and to effect regime change. USA and allies become bogged down in protracted insurgency lasting eight years but country remained unstable thereafter.

2010 – Arab Spring. A series of civil uprisings arose across North Africa and the Middle East triggered by a mix of general unrest at authoritarian governments, corruption and poverty. Some uprisings simply fizzled out whilst others effected regime change and some (notably Syria, Libya and Yemen) produced extended civil war.

2011 – Fukushima (Japan) nuclear accident. An offshore earthquake triggered normal safety shutdown but subsequent 14-metre-high tsunami flooded reactors and shut down emergency power for cooling water. Three reactor meltdowns and explosions resulted with major release of radiation inside a 20 km exclusion zone.

2014 – Ebola Virus Disease (EVD) epidemic arises in W Africa. Over 11,000 deaths.

Russian Annexation of Crimea. After the Ukraine government was overthrown for refusing political association and a free-trade agreement with the EU, Russia invades then annexes Crimea. Claimed basis was to achieve self-determination for Crimean citizens but Russian access to potential oil and gas reserves may have played a part. The UN condemns the annexation.

2015 – European migrant crisis. Large numbers of people begin seeking asylum in Northern Europe from either poor or war-torn countries in Northern Africa and the Middle East. EU countries become stretched in their ability to absorb them and because of unequal political approaches within EU. People smuggling and trafficking become rampant.

2020 – Covid 19 virus, first detected in Wuhan (*China*) in December 2019, spreads rapidly throughout the world, being declared a pandemic three months later. Severity varied but the virus proved potentially fatal and triggered a rush to develop and distribute an effective vaccine.

The United Kingdom formally withdraws from the European Union (EU).

2022 – Covid-19 virus continues to spread rapidly throughout the world, threatening to overwhelm established health services.

Russia invades Ukraine in what it claims is a "limited military operation" and encounters fierce resistance and international condemnation. Western powers (primarily USA, UK and EU) support Ukraine financially and with supplies of advanced weaponry. International trade in grain, oil and gas is disrupted.

Global average inflation rises to 7.4% (from 4.35% in 2021). **2023** – Russian attacks on Ukraine continue with few territorial gains. International grain, oil and gas shortages develop, together with continuing widespread economic inflation.

Vaccination programs prove largely successful in limiting the continued Covid-19 pandemic but widespread deaths and illness continue, notably in China.

Palestinian militants in Gaza launch a surprise attack on adjacent Israeli settlements killing some 1,100 and taking over 200 hostages. Israel responds with widespread bombing and shelling of Gaza and a complete blockade of food, water, and electricity. Over 20,000 Gazan deaths result, primarily innocent civilians while Israel, with US support, ignores UN demands for a humanitarian ceasefire. Israeli raids and arrests of Palestinians in other occupied areas increase, as do attacks by Israelis illegally (by international norms) settling on Palestinian land.

History is much like a diamond with an infinite number of facets. I have addressed those I thought significant in terms of mankind's progress but have doubtless missed or ignored many more that the reader may consider fundamental. Mea Culpa! Indeed, each facet addressed has a myriad more warranting further examination, although accommodating them would be well beyond the scope of this work and take up many libraries to encompass. I have been anxious to avoid producing a book that weighs as much as a brick.

I salute the many chroniclers of history over the ages and acknowledge that this book relies on their many endeavours without attribution. There were simply too many sources of the facts herein to list individually – a task that would more than double the size of this volume and in any event was beyond my capacity to keep up. The reader may be assured, though, that each stated event was checked and re-checked from multiple independent sources. Those sources often differed in detail: where they did, I have made considered judgements but, of course, consequent errors are mine own.

Abandoning my avoidance of attributions, I feel mention must be made of my occasional reference to "*Wikipedia*". Whilst not always an authoritative source and often denounced in academe, it is free, readily accessible and provides a very handy check on obscure detail, spelling and miscellaneous references. It is a worthy 21st Century addition to any historian's toolbox or the local library and I commend any provision of donations for its ongoing availability. Quoting it as a source in any formal academic work, though, is tempting fate (and censure!).

An almost inevitable feature of historical commentary written in the English language is a bias toward those aspects affecting the English-speaking world itself. I have tried to avoid that, though not always successfully. Equally, I am conscious of having taken liberties with references to "English" as opposed to "British", for which a change was effected in 1707. Even that latter term fails to acknowledge the citizens of Northern Ireland, so until someone coins an acceptable collective term for the citizens of the United Kingdom, then I trust that some latitude may be permitted.

There are some persons of an extremist academic bent who regard any use of a word incorporating "man" ("mankind", "sportsmanship" etc) as offensively non-inclusive. Maybe a future world will have better terminology and accommodate more inclusiveness and diversity, but for now mankind remains overwhelmingly binary. In my usage, "mankind" includes males and females as well as those that assert gender neutrality.

www.ingramcontent.com/pod-product-compliance
Lightning Source LLC
Chambersburg PA
CBHW050334160726
48002CB00001B/306